Understanding
and Facilitating
Forgiveness

Understanding and Facilitating Forgiveness

Strategic Pastoral Counseling Resources

David G. Benner
and Robert W. Harvey

Baker Books

A Division of Baker Book House Co
Grand Rapids, Michigan 49516

Published by Baker Books
a division of Baker Book House Company
P.O. Box 6287, Grand Rapids, MI 49516–6287

Printed in the United States of America

Library of Congress Cataloging-in-Publication Data

Benner, David G.
    Understanding and facilitating forgiveness / David G. Benner and Robert W. Harvey.
        p. cm. — (Strategic pastoral counseling resources)
    Includes bibliographical references.
    ISBN 0-8010-9019-9
    1. Forgiveness—Religious aspects—Christianity. 2. Pastoral counseling. I. Harvey, Robert W. II. Title. III. Series.
BV4647.F55B46 1996
234′.5—dc20
                                              96-15340

Contents

Preface (Series Preface)   7

Part One: Understanding Forgiveness

1.   The Importance of Forgiveness   25
2.   The Possibility of Forgiveness   41
3.   The Necessity of Forgiveness   57
4.   The Difficulty of Forgiveness   71

Part Two: Facilitating Forgiveness

5.   The Role of Forgiveness in Pastoral Care   87
6.   Case Study I   101
7.   Case Study II   127
8.   Case Study III   139

Notes   159

5

An Introduction to Strategic Pastoral Counseling

David G. Benner

While the provision of spiritual counsel has been an integral part of Christian soul care since the earliest days of the church, the contemporary understanding and practice of pastoral counseling is largely a product of the twentieth century. Developing within the shadow of the modern psychotherapies, pastoral counseling has derived much of its style and approach from these clinical therapeutics. What this has meant is that pastoral counselors have often seen themselves more as counselors than as pastors and the counseling that they have provided has often been a rather awkward adaptation of clinical counseling models to a pastoral context. This, in turn, has often resulted in significant tension between the pastoral and psychological dimensions of the counseling provided by clergy and others in Christian ministry. It is also frequently reflected in pastoral counselors who are more interested in anything connected with the modern mystery cult of psychotherapy than with their own tradition of Christian soul care, and who, as a consequence, are often quite insecure in their pastoral role and identity.

7

While pastoral counseling owes much to the psychological culture that has gained ascendancy in the West during the past century, this influence has quite clearly been a mixed blessing. Contemporary pastoral counselors typically offer their help with much more psychological sophistication than was the case several decades ago, but all too often they do so without a clear sense of the uniqueness of counseling that is offered by a pastor. And not only are the distinctive spiritual resources of Christian ministry often deemphasized or ignored, but the tensions that are associated with attempts to directly translate clinical models of counseling into the pastoral context become a source of much frustration. This is in part why so many pastors report dissatisfaction with their counseling. While they indicate that this dissatisfaction is a result of insufficient training in and time for counseling, a bigger part of the problem may be that pastors have been offered approaches to counseling that are of questionable appropriateness for the pastoral context and that will inevitably leave them feeling frustrated and inadequate.

Strategic Pastoral Counseling is a model of counseling that has been specifically designed to fit the role, resources, and needs of the typical pastor who counsels. Information about this "typical" pastor was solicited by means of a survey of over 400 pastors (this research is described in the introductory volume of the series, *Strategic Pastoral Counseling: A Short-Term Structured Model* [Benner 1992]). The model appropriates the insights of contemporary counseling theory without sacrificing the resources of pastoral ministry. Furthermore, it takes its form and direction from the pastoral role and in so doing offers an approach to counseling that is not only congruent with the other aspects of pastoral ministry but that places pastoral counseling at the very heart of ministry.

The present volume represents an application of Strategic Pastoral Counseling to one commonly encountered problem situation. As such, it presupposes a familiarity with the basic model. Readers not familiar with *Strategic Pastoral Counseling: A Short-Term Structured Model* should consult that book for a detailed presentation of the model and its implementation. What follows is a brief review of this material which, while it does not adequately summarize all that is presented in that book, should serve as a reminder of the most important features of the Strategic Pastoral Counseling approach.

The Strategic Pastoral Counseling Model

Strategic Pastoral Counseling is short-term, bibliotherapeutic, wholistic, structured, spiritually focused, and explicitly Christian. Each of these characteristics will be briefly discussed in order.

Short-Term Counseling

Counseling can be brief (that is, conducted over a relatively few sessions), time-limited (that is, conducted within an initially fixed number of total sessions), or both. Strategic Pastoral Counseling is both brief and time-limited, working within a suggested maximum of five sessions. The decision to set this upper limit on the number of sessions was in response to the fact that the background research conducted in the design of the model indicated that 87 percent of the pastoral counseling conducted by pastors in general ministry involves five sessions or less. This short-term approach to counseling seems ideally suited to the time availability, training, and role demands of pastors.

Recent research in short-term counseling has made it clear that while such an approach requires that the counselor be diligent in maintaining the focus on the single agreed upon central problem, significant and enduring changes can occur through a very small number of counseling sessions. Strategic Pastoral Counseling differs, in this regard, from the more ongoing relationship of discipleship or spiritual guidance. In these, the goal is the development of spiritual maturity. Strategic Pastoral Counseling has a much more modest goal: examining a particular problem or experience in the light of God's will for and activity in the life of the individual seeking help and attempting to facilitate growth in and through that person's present life situation. While this is still an ambitious goal, its focused nature makes it quite attainable within a short period of time. It is this focus that makes the counseling strategic.

The five-session limit should be communicated by the pastor no later than the first session and preferably in the prior conversation when the time is set for this session. This ensures that the parishioner is aware of the time limit from the beginning and can share responsibility in keeping the counseling sessions focused. Some people will undoubtedly require more than five sessions in order to bring about a resolution of their problems. These people should be referred to someone who is appropriately qualified for such work; preparation for this referral will be one of the goals of the five sessions. However, the fact that such people may require more help than can be provided in five sessions of pastoral counseling does not mean that they cannot benefit from such focused short-term pastoral care; no individuals should be regarded as inappropriate candidates for Strategic Pastoral Counseling merely because they may require other help.

One final but important note about the suggested limit of five sessions is that this does not have to be tied to a corresponding period of five weeks. In fact, many pastors find weekly sessions to be less useful than sessions scheduled two or three weeks apart. This sort of spacing of the last couple of sessions is particularly helpful and should be considered even if the first several sessions are held weekly.

Bibliotherapeutic Counseling

Bibliotherapy refers to the therapeutic use of reading. Strategic Pastoral Counseling builds the use of written materials into the heart of its approach to pastoral caregiving. The Bible itself is, of course, a rich bibliotherapeutic resource and the encouragement of and direction in its reading is an important part of Strategic Pastoral Counseling. Its use must be disciplined and selective and particular care must be taken to ensure that it is never employed in a mechanical or impersonal manner. However, when used appropriately it can unquestionably be one of the most dynamic and powerful resources available to the pastor who counsels.

While the Bible is a unique bibliotherapeutic resource, it is not the only such resource. Strategic Pastoral Counseling comes with a built-in set of specifically designed resources. Each of the 10 volumes in this series has an accompanying book written for the parishioner who is being seen in counseling. These resource books are written by the same authors as the volumes for pastors and are designed for easy integration into counseling sessions.

The use of reading materials that are consistent with the counseling being provided can serve as a most significant support and extension of the counseling offered by a pastor. The parishioner now has a helping resource that is not limited by the pastor's time and availability. Furthermore, the pastor can now allow the written materials to do part of the work of counseling, using the sessions to deal with those matters that are not as well addressed through the written page.

Wholistic Counseling

It might seem surprising to suggest that a short-term counseling approach should also be wholistic. But this is both possible and highly desirable. Wholistic counseling is counseling that is responsive to the totality of the complex psycho-spiritual dynamics that make up the life of human persons. Biblical psychology is clearly a wholistic psychology. The various "parts" of persons (i.e., body, soul, spirit, heart, flesh, etc.) are never presented as separate faculties or independent components of persons but always as different ways of seeing the whole person. Biblical discussions of persons emphasize first and foremost their essential unity of being. Humans are ultimately understandable only in the light of this primary and irreducible wholeness, and helping efforts that are truly Christian must resist the temptation to see persons only through their thoughts, feelings, behaviors, or any other single manifestation of being.

The alternative to wholism in counseling is to focus on only one of these modalities of functioning and this is, indeed, what many approaches to counseling do. In contrast, Strategic Pastoral Counseling asserts that pastoral counseling must be responsive to the behavioral (action), cognitive (thought), and affective (feeling) elements of personal functioning. Each examined separately can obscure that which is really going on with a person. But taken together they form the basis for a comprehensive assessment and effective intervention. Strategic Pastoral Counseling provides a framework for ensuring that each of these spheres of functioning is addressed and this, in fact, provides much of the structure for the counseling.

Structured Counseling

The structured nature of Strategic Pastoral Counseling is that which enables its brevity, ensuring that each of the sessions has a clear focus and that each builds upon the previous ones in contributing toward the accomplishment of the overall goals. The framework that structures Strategic Pastoral Counseling is sufficiently tight as to enable the pastor to provide a wholistic assessment and counseling intervention within a maximum of five sessions and yet it is also sufficiently flexible to allow for differences in individual styles of different counselors. This is very important because Strategic Pastoral Counseling is not primarily a set of techniques but an intimate encounter of and dialogue between people.

The structure of Strategic Pastoral Counseling grows out of the goal of addressing the feelings, thoughts, and behaviors that are part of the troubling experiences of the person seeking help. It is also a structure that is responsive to the several tasks that face the pastoral counselor, tasks such as conducting an initial assessment, developing a general understanding of the problem and of the person's major needs, and selecting and delivering interventions and resources that will bring help. This structure is described in more detail later.

Spiritually Focused Counseling

The fourth distinctive of Strategic Pastoral Counseling is that it is spiritually focused. This does not mean that only religious matters are discussed. Our spirituality is our essential heart commitments, our basic life direction, and our fundamental allegiances. These spiritual aspects of our being are, of course, reflected in our attitudes toward God and are expressed in our explicitly religious values and behaviors. However, they are also reflected in matters that may seem on the surface to be much less religious. Strategic Pastoral Counselors place a primacy on listening to this underlying spiritual story. They listen for what we might call the story behind the story.

But listening to the story behind the story requires that one first listen to and take seriously the presenting story. To disregard the presenting situation is spiritualization of a problem. It fails to take the problem seriously and makes a mockery of counseling as genuine dialogue. The Strategic Pastoral Counselor thus listens to and enters into the experience of parishioners as they relate their struggles and life's experiences. But while this is a real part of the story, it is not the whole story that must be heard and understood. For in the midst of this story emerges another: the story of their spiritual response to these experiences. This response may be one of unwavering trust in God but a failure to expect much of him. Or it may be one of doubt, anger, confusion, or despair. Each of these is a spiritual response to present struggles and in one form or another, the spiritual aspect of the person's experience will always be discernible to the pastor who watches for it. Strategic Pastoral Counseling makes this underlying spiritual story the primary focus.

Explicitly Christian Counseling

While it is important to not confuse spirituality with religiosity, it is equally important to not confuse Christian spirituality with any of its imitations. In this regard, it is crucial that Strategic Pastoral Counseling be distinctively and explicitly Christian. And while Strategic Pastoral Counseling begins with a focus on spiritual matters understood broadly, its master goal is to facilitate the other person's awareness of and response to the call of God to surrender and service. This is the essential and most important distinctive of Strategic Pastoral Counseling.

One of the ways in which Strategic Pastoral Counseling is made explicitly Christian is through its utilization of Christian theological language, images, and concepts and the religious resources of prayer, Scripture, and the sacraments. These resources must never be used in a mechanical, legalistic, or magical fashion. But used sensitively and wisely, they can be the conduit for a dynamic contact between God and the person seeking pastoral help. And this is the goal of their utilization, not some superficial baptizing of the counseling in order to make it Christian but rather a way of bringing the one seeking help more closely in touch with the God who is the source of all life, growth, and healing.

Another important resource that is appropriated by the Strategic Pastoral Counselor is that of the church as a community. Too often pastoral counseling is conducted in a way that is not appreciably different from that which might be offered by a Christian counselor in private practice. This most unfortunate practice ignores the rich resources that are potentially available in any Christian congregation. One of the most important ways in which Strategic Pastoral Counseling is able to maintain its short-term nature is by the pastor connecting the person seeking help with others in the church who can provide portions of that help. The congregation can, of course, also be involved in less individualistic ways. Support and ministry groups of various sorts are becoming a part of many congregations that seek to provide a dynamic ministry to their community and are potentially important resources for the Strategic Pastoral Counselor.

A final and even more fundamental way in which Strategic Pastoral Counseling is Christian is in the reliance that it encourages on the Holy Spirit. The Spirit is the indispensable source of all wisdom that is necessary for the practice of pastoral counseling. Recognizing that all healing and growth are ultimately of God, the Strategic Pastoral Counselor can thus take comfort in this reliance on the Spirit of God and on the fact that ultimate responsibility for people and their well-being lies with God.

Stages and Tasks of Strategic Pastoral Counseling

The three overall stages that organize Strategic Pastoral Counseling can be described as *encounter, engagement,* and *disengagement.* The first stage of Strategic Pastoral Counseling, encounter, corresponds to the initial session in which the goal is to establish personal contact with the person seeking help, set the boundaries for the counseling relationship, become acquainted with that person and the central concerns, conduct a pastoral diagnosis, and develop a mutually acceptable focus for the subsequent sessions. The second stage, engagement, involves the pastor moving beyond the first contact and establishing a deeper working alliance with the person seeking help. This normally occupies the next one to three sessions and entails the exploration of the person's feelings, thoughts, and behavioral patterns associated with this problem area and the development of new perspectives and strategies for coping or change. The third and final stage, disengagement, describes the focus of the last one or possibly two sessions, and involves an evaluation of progress and an assessment of remaining concerns, the making of a referral for further help if this is needed, and the ending of the counseling relationship. These stages and tasks are summarized in the table below.

Stages and Tasks of Strategic Pastoral Counseling

Stage 1: Encounter (Session 1)
* Joining and boundary-setting
* Exploring the central concerns and relevant history
* Conducting a pastoral diagnosis
* Achieving a mutually agreeable focus for counseling

Stage 2: Engagement (Sessions 2, 3, 4)
* Exploration of cognitive, affective, and behavioral aspects of the problem and the identification of resources for coping or change

Stage 3: Disengagement (Sessions 4, 5)
* Evaluation of progress and assessment of remaining concerns
* Referral (if needed)
* Termination of counseling

The Encounter Stage

The first task in this initial stage of Strategic Pastoral Counseling is joining and boundary-setting. Joining involves putting the parishioner at ease by means of a few moments of casual conversation that is designed to ease pastor and parishioner into contact. Such preliminary conversation should never take more than five minutes and should usually be kept to two or three. It will not always be necessary, because some people are immediately ready to tell their story. Boundary-setting involves the communication of the purpose of this session and the time frame for the session and your work together. This should not normally require more than a sentence or two.

The exploration of central concerns and relevant history usually begins with an invitation for parishioners to describe what led them to seek help at the present time. After hearing an expression of these immediate concerns, it is usually helpful to get a brief historical perspective on these concerns and the person. Ten to 15 minutes of exploration of the course of development of the presenting problems and their efforts to cope or get help with them is the foundation of this part of the session. It is also important at this point to get some idea of the parishioner's present living and family arrangements as well as work and/or educational situation. The organizing thread for this section of the first interview should be the presenting problem. These matters will not be the only ones discussed but this focus serves to give the session the necessary direction.

Stripped of its distracting medical connotations, diagnosis is problem definition and this is a fundamental part of any approach to counseling. Diagnoses involve judgments about the nature of the problem and, either implicitly or explicitly, pastoral counselors make such judgments every time they commence a counseling relationship. But in order for diagnoses to be relevant they must guide the counseling that will follow. This means that the categories of pastoral assessment must be primarily related to the spiritual focus, which is foundational to any counseling that is appropriately called pastoral. Thus, the diagnosis called for in the first stage of Strategic Pastoral Counseling involves an assessment of the person's spiritual well-being.

The framework for pastoral diagnosis adopted by Strategic Pastoral Counseling is that suggested by Malony (1988) and used as the basis of his Religious Status Interview. Malony proposed that the diagnosis of Christian religious well-being should involve the assessment of the person's awareness of God, acceptance of God's grace, repentance and responsibility, response to God's leadership and direction, involvement in the church, experience of fellowship, ethics, and openness in the faith. While this approach to pastoral diagnosis has been found to be helpful by many, the Strategic Pastoral Counselor need not feel confined by it. It is offered as a suggested framework for conducting a pastoral assessment and each individual pastoral counselor needs to approach this task in ways that fit his or her own theological convictions and personal style. Further details on conducting a pastoral assessment can be found in *Strategic Pastoral Counseling: A Short-Term Structured Model.*

The final task of the encounter stage of Strategic Pastoral Counseling is achieving a mutually agreeable focus for counseling. Often this is self-evident, made immediately clear by the first expression of the parishioner. At other times parishioners will report a wide range of concerns in the first session and will have to be asked what should constitute the primary problem focus. The identification of the primary problem focus leads naturally to a formulation of goals for the counseling. These goals will sometimes be quite specific (i.e., to be able to make an informed decision about a potential job change) but will also at times be rather broad (i.e., to be able to express feelings related to an illness). As is illustrated in these examples, some goals will describe an end-point while others will describe more of a process. Maintaining this flexibility in how goals are understood is crucial if Strategic Pastoral Counseling is to be a helpful counseling approach for the broad range of situations faced by the pastoral counselor.

The Engagement Stage

The second stage of Strategic Pastoral Counseling involves the further engagement of the pastor and the one seeking help around the problems and concerns that brought them together. This is the heart of the counseling process. The major tasks of this stage are the exploration of the person's feelings, thoughts, and behavioral patterns associated with the central concerns and the development of new perspectives and strategies for coping or change.

It is important to note that the work of this stage may well begin in the first session. The model should not be interpreted in a rigid or mechanical manner. If the goals of the first stage are completed with time remaining in the first session, one can very appropriately begin to move into the tasks of this next stage. However, once the tasks of Stage 1 are completed, those associated with this second stage become the central focus. If the full five sessions of Strategic Pastoral Counseling are employed, this second stage normally provides the structure for sessions 2, 3, and 4.

The central foci for the three sessions normally associated with this stage are the feelings, thoughts, and behaviors associated with the problem presented by the person seeking help. Although these are usually intertwined, a selective focus on each, one at a time, ensures that each is adequately addressed and that all the crucial dynamics of the person's psychospiritual functioning are considered.

The reason for beginning with feelings is that this is where most people themselves begin when they come to a counselor. But this does not mean that most people know their feelings. The exploration of feelings involves encouraging people to face and express whatever it is that they are feeling, to the end that these feelings can be known and then dealt with appropriately. The goal at this point is to listen and respond empathically to the feelings of those seeking help, not to try to change them.

After an exploration of the major feelings being experienced by the person seeking help, the next task is an exploration of the thoughts associated with these feelings and the development of alternative ways of understanding present experiences. It is in this phase of Strategic Pastoral Counseling that the explicit use of Scripture is usually most appropriate. Bearing in mind the potential misuses and problems that can be associated with such use of religious resources, the pastoral counselor should be, nonetheless, open to a direct presentation of scriptural truths when they offer the possibility of a new and helpful perspective on one's situation.

The final task of the engagement stage of Strategic Pastoral Counseling grows directly out of this work on understanding and involves the exploration of the behavioral components of the person's functioning. Here the pastor explores what concrete things the person is doing in the face of the problems or distressing situations being encountered and together with the parishioner begins to identify changes in behavior that may be desirable. The goal of this stage is to identify changes that both pastor and parishioner agree are important and to begin to establish concrete strategies for making these changes.

The Disengagement Stage

The last session or two involves preparation for the termination of counseling and includes two specific tasks: the evaluation of progress and assessment of remaining concerns, and making arrangements regarding a referral if this is needed.

The evaluation of progress is usually a process that both pastor and parishioner will find rewarding. Some of this may be done during previous sessions. Even when this is the case, it is a good idea to use the last session to undertake a brief review of what has been learned from the counseling. Closely associated with this, of course, is an identification of remaining concerns. Seldom is everything resolved after five sessions. This means that the parishioner is preparing to leave counseling with some work yet to be done. But he or she does so with plans for the future and the development of these is an important task of the disengagement stage of Strategic Pastoral Counseling.

If significant problems remain at this point, the last couple of sessions should also be used to make referral arrangements. Ideally these should be discussed in the second or third session and they should by now be all arranged. It might even be ideal if by this point the parishioner could have had a first session with the new counselor, thus allowing a processing of this first experience as part of the final pastoral counseling session.

Recognition of one's own limitations of time, experience, training, and ability is an indispensable component of the practice of all professionals. Pastors are no exception. Pastors offering Strategic Pastoral Counseling need, therefore, to be aware of the resources within their community and be prepared to refer parishioners for help that they can better receive elsewhere.

In the vast majority of cases, the actual termination of a Strategic Pastoral Counseling relationship goes very smoothly. Most often both pastor and parishioner agree that there is no further need to meet and they find easy agreement with, even if some sadness around, the decision to discontinue the counseling sessions. However, there may be times when this process is somewhat difficult. This will sometimes be due to the parishioner's desire to continue to meet. At other times the difficulty in terminating will reside within the pastor. Regardless, the best course of action is usually to follow through on the initial limits agreed upon by both parties.

The exception to this rule is a situation where the parishioner is facing some significant stress or crisis at the end of the five sessions and where there are no other available resources to provide the support needed. If this is the situation, an extension of a few sessions may be appropriate. However, this should again be time-limited and should take the form of crisis management. It should not involve more sessions than is absolutely necessary to restore some degree of stability or to introduce the parishioner to other people who can be of assistance.

Conclusion

Strategic Pastoral Counseling provides a framework for pastors who seek to counsel in a way that is congruent with the rest of their pastoral responsibilities, psychologically informed and responsible. While skill in implementing the model comes only over time, because the approach is focused and time-limited it is quite possible for most pastors to acquire these skills. However, counseling skills cannot be adequately learned simply by reading books. As with all interpersonal skills, they must be learned through practice, and ideally, this practice is best acquired in a context of supervisory feedback from a more experienced pastoral counselor.

The pastor who has mastered the skills of Strategic Pastoral Counseling is in a position to proclaim the Word of God in a highly personalized and relevant manner to people who are often desperate for help. This is a unique and richly rewarding opportunity. Rather than scattering seed in a broadcast manner across ground that is often stony and hard even if at places it is also fertile and receptive to growth, the pastoral counselor has the opportunity to carefully plant one seed at a time. Knowing the soil conditions, he or she is also able to plant it in a highly individualized manner, taking pains to ensure that it will not be quickly blown away, and then gently watering and nourishing its growth. This is the unique opportunity for the ministry of Strategic Pastoral Counseling. It is my prayer that pastors will see the centrality of counseling to their call to ministry, feel encouraged by the presence of an approach to pastoral counseling that lies within their skills and time availability, and will take up these responsibilities with renewed vigor and clarity of direction.

Part **1**

Understanding Forgiveness

The Importance of Forgiveness

T he single most important concept in biblical Christianity is forgiveness. Throughout both Old and New Testaments, we are presented with the supreme value of divine forgiveness of our sins and are repeatedly enjoined to forgive others for their sins against us. Jesus linked these two expressions of forgiveness to each other in his declaration that "if you forgive men when they sin against you, your heavenly Father will also forgive you. But if you do not forgive men their sins, your Father will not forgive your sins" (Matt. 6:14–15). It would be hard to imagine how Jesus could have given the topic of forgiveness any more emphasis than this.

The Bible presents forgiveness as a prospect so desirable that it seems to loom as the most essential experience for wholeness in life. Consider some of the vivid images with which biblical authors portray the blessing of receiving God's forgiving grace.

Forgiveness produces:

A sense of cleanness: David prays longingly, "Wash away all my iniquity and cleanse me from my sin . . . cleanse me . . . and I will be clean, wash me, and I will be whiter than snow" (Ps. 51:2, 7). God counters Satan's accusations against Joshua the high priest by commanding that Joshua's filthy clothes (symbolic of sin) be removed by an angel and clean clothes given to him, saying, "See, I have taken away your sin. . . ." (Zech. 3:1–5).

A sense of guilt decisively removed: King Hezekiah felt the authority with which God had declared him forgiven, "You have put all my sins behind your back" (Isa. 38:17). The prophet Micah anticipated God's thorough removal of guilt, "Who is a God like you, who pardons sin and forgives . . . You will tread our sins underfoot and hurl all our iniquities into the depths of the sea" (Micah 7:18–19). God declared his power to remove sin's condemnation to Israel. "I have swept away your offenses like a cloud, your sins like the morning mist" (Isa. 44:22).

A sense of healing and emotional release: "But for you who revere my name, the sun of righteousness will rise with healing in its wings. And you will go out and leap like calves released from the stall" (Mal. 4:2).

A new clarity of mind about God's purpose: "I pray also that the eyes of your heart may be enlightened in order that you may know the hope to which he has called you, the riches of his glorious inheritance in the saints, and his incomparably great power for us who believe" (Eph. 1:18–19).

A new unity between persons: "How good and pleasant it is when brothers dwell together in unity! It is like precious oil poured on the head, running down . . . It is like the dew. . . ." (Ps. 133). Reconciled persons experience the pleasure of new beginnings ("dew") and new attractiveness to one another (sweet smelling, glistening oil in the hair).

Forgiveness is a freeing, empowering, refreshing, healing, and joyful experience which is capable of transforming all of life. Therefore, the failure to forgive or be forgiven means the loss of much or all of this emotional health from one's experience. This tragic cost of the failure of forgiveness is also graphically portrayed in Scripture.

An absence of forgiveness produces:

A clinging sense of uncleanness and lostness: ". . . all our righteous acts are like filthy rags; we all shrivel up like a leaf and like the wind our sins sweep us away" (Isa. 64:6).

A sense of unresolved guilt: ". . . my sin is always before me" (Ps. 51:3).

A continuing sense of woundedness and longing for healing: "I am feeble and utterly crushed; I groan in anguish of heart" (Ps. 38:8). "Let me hear joy and gladness; let the bones you have crushed rejoice" (Ps. 51:8).

Darkness of mind and confusion about God's purpose: "He feeds on ashes, a deluded heart misleads him . . . We look for light, but all is darkness; for brightness, but we walk in deep shadows. Like the blind we grope along the wall . . . at midday we stumble. . . ." (Isa. 44:20; 59:9–10).

A growing disunity between persons even within the Christian fellowship: "If you keep biting and devouring each other, watch out or you will be destroyed by each other" (Gal. 5:15).

There is a chronic anger that grows from the failure to forgive and there is an anger that festers beneath the failure to seek or accept forgiveness. Dan Allender speaks of this in connection with his discussion of the dynamics of abuse, shame, and feelings of contempt.

> Contempt is condemnation, an attack against the perceived cause of the shame. The attack is laced with hatred, venom, and cruelty, though it can be as insidious as a warm smile and gentle rebuke. The condemnation can be against the person whose eyes are penetrating our facade or against the element of our being that is the cause of the shameful revelation.
>
> Shame is a phenomenon of the eyes. The eyes usually drop and the shoulders slump when one feels shame. More than anything in the world the shamed person wants to be invisible or small so that the focus will be removed, the hemorrhage of the soul stopped. How can the shamed person accomplish this? Somehow the eyes of the one who sees him must be deflected or destroyed. And there are two options. The shamed person can turn his eyes away from the penetrating gaze and focus on the element in his own being that is the cause of the shame. Or he can attack his "enemy's" eyes directly with the poison of his hatred, blinding those eyes so their power is nullified. The first option, self-contempt, and the second, other-centered contempt, though different in form, are similar in function.[1]

The damage which results from a lack of forgiveness is tremendous. Both individuals, the Christian community of which they are a part, and their families and friends all may suffer deeply. Forgiveness involves even more than the healing of our relationships. Scripture also presents evidence for a link between forgiveness and health. David spoke of his "bones wasting away" and his "strength being sapped" until he finally confessed his sins and received God's forgiveness (Ps. 32:3–4). Similar symptoms appear to be his experience connected to guilt in Psalm 38: "My guilt overwhelmed me . . . My back is filled with searing pain; there is no health in my body . . . My heart pounds, my strength fails me. . . ." (vv. 4, 7, 10). Jesus also demonstrated the close connection between forgiveness and physical health in his cure of the paralytic who was healed as a result of Jesus forgiving his sin (Matt. 9:1–8).

This close connection between forgiveness and health has recently also been noted by medical researchers. Recent research has shown that the experience of receiving forgiveness strengthens the body's immune system and helps us ward off or heal more rapidly from disease. On the other hand, people who have a tendency to hold resentment and a related inability to forgive others are much more likely to develop a range of diseases, including cancer and heart disease. An even more direct risk to physical life has been noted by psychiatrist E. Mansell Pattison, who suggests that murder typifies the ultimate failure to forgive another, and suicide, the ultimate failure to forgive oneself.[2] A failure to forgive others and the accompanying resentment and bitterness, has also been reported to be the leading cause of burnout.

In light of the destructiveness of resentment and the healing nature of forgiveness, it is important that we forgive others for their offenses against us as quickly as possible. Resentment is a poison that destroys our body, soul, and spirit, and we should, therefore, strive to neutralize this poison with the antidote of forgiveness as soon as we are able. The inability to accept forgiveness is also equally destructive. Thus, how vital is our pastoral ministry of the forgiving grace of God! Forgiveness is an unmerited gift through the sacrificial atonement accomplished by Jesus Christ. It is God's offer of health and wholeness.

Richard Ecker quotes a fellow participant in a ministerial con-ference, "I have talked with a lot of hurting people over the years. With few exceptions, they all were solidly in touch with the extent of their sins. Where they needed help was getting in touch with the grace of God." Ecker adds, "If I had to specify the most fundamen-tal deficiency in emotional dysfunction, it would be the inability to experience the unconditional. To the emotionally disabled, grace—unconditional love—is a totally foreign concept, at least at the gut level where it counts. This is because their personalities have been shaped so totally by programming that makes value conditional."[3] Thus the church must be the place where in counsel and in con-gregational life, those emotionally disabled by unforgiveness and conditional acceptance will experience grace through faith in Christ.

Every pastor must realize how vital this is, not only to the heal-ing and wholeness of individuals but also to the health, purity, peace, and unity of the whole congregation under their care. Con-sider a case example:

Terri asked her pastor for counsel, indicating that she felt her marriage was severely threatened. This surprised the pastor, for he had recognized no signs of tension between Terri and her husband. They had a reputation among the young married couples in the con-gregation, a reputation for being deeply in love. They always stood with arms around each other, sat in church as close together as physically possible, usually with her head resting on his shoulder. Now she sat in the pastor's study trying to control sobbing and tears which had made it impossible to talk. Her torment came out in a wail of hopelessness, "I can't stand it any longer. But he can't love me if I tell him—he'll hate me!"

Gradually her story unfolded, her pain coming from years of fear that her husband would discover that she had been sexually active long before their marriage. The guilt that now seemed to consume her came from sins committed in her early youth, years before she became a Christian. She was, indeed, now very much a different person, faithful in marriage, unable to imagine being attracted to another man, yet tormented by sins long ago confessed to God.

Her needs certainly began with her lack of understanding of the implications of God's grace for her through her faith in the Savior whom she already loved. And in the days which followed she did begin to find release from the guilt which had been like a rusty iron band clamped around her heart. She had long heard that for anyone in Christ "the old has gone, the new has come" (2 Cor. 5:17), but she had feared that only certain "old things" were forgivable and that others—her youthful sexual experiments—were not. Now she began to dare to believe herself to be truly a new person in Christ, as she learned the realities of forgiveness. There were as yet unresolved questions: Did her husband need to know of those sins committed so long before she met him? Would she need to confess to him in order to make her freedom from the past complete? Would he be able to forgive her through the same grace from God which was now giving her such a new sense of wholeness? How many "Terris" were there in that congregation? How many Christians troubled by the desperate need to know forgiveness? Will we be ready to help them if they come to us, their teachers in the school of grace?

Forgiveness as a Hard-Work Miracle

While forgiveness involves great effort, these efforts do not produce forgiveness. Forgiveness is something that we do by a free act of our will, but the ability to forgive is a gift, we might even say a miracle.

This should not be understood as in any way minimizing the effort that is required. As noted by David Augsburger, "True forgiveness is the hardest thing in the universe." No human action is more difficult than genuine forgiveness. Nothing more difficult will ever be asked of any human than to forgive someone who hurt them. However, the release of anger and the healing of damaged emotions that comes from forgiveness is not something that I produce by my efforts. I do the hard work that is my part and then I receive the wonderful gift of forgiveness. It is something, therefore, that I should receive with gratitude.

Forgiveness requires that we do our part and then we ask God to do his part. His part is in helping us release the anger and then in giving us the resulting emotional freedom and healing. I don't simply pray to God that he will render the other person forgiven by me. Unfortunately, it is not that easy. But I can and should pray that God would help me forgive the other person. This is a prayer he will answer because it is clearly something that he wills for me.

But it is here that we need to note the relationship between receiving forgiveness and giving it. As it is hard to imagine how one could ever give love if he or she had never received love from another, so too it is hard to imagine how someone could forgive another if he or she had never received forgiveness themselves. Knowing myself to be one who has needed and received forgiveness allows me to grant others this great and undeserved gift. And supremely, knowing myself to have needed and received the forgiveness of God allows me to become a forgiving person in a way that is quite impossible when only dealing with the experience of forgiveness as received from the hands of fellow humans. "God's forgiveness toward me and my forgiveness toward another are like the voice and the echo."[4] Without the former, the latter is both impossible and a meaningless absurdity.

Forgiveness is always a gift, a grace. I become capable of giving forgiveness because I have already received it. I didn't have to earn it from those who gave it to me and similarly, those who hurt me can do nothing to earn it from me. Forgiveness is, in essence, a gift of unearned extravagance and generosity.

Nothing in the world bears the imprint of the Son of God as clearly as forgiveness. Jesus Christ the incarnate Son of God is the greatest miracle of all possible miracles; he is the wondrous, gracious coming of God himself to us to rescue us from guilt and death and bestow upon us the incomparable gift of new life, present and eternal. We may reverently say that the incarnation is a miracle even beyond that of the creation when God spoke a word and the universe sprang into existence (2 Peter 3:5). We may also say that the work he accomplished, the work of redemption was a work of difficulty beyond any ever conceived in history (Isa. 63:3; Heb. 9:9, 14). If, in our human experience, we are able to forgive "as in Christ God forgave" us (Eph. 4:32), then our acts of forgiveness will bear the impress of the Great Forgiver; they will be both miraculous and difficult, they will be indeed "hard-work miracles."

But perhaps we tend to believe in the hard work of forgiveness more than we believe in or expect it as a miracle of grace. It is so hard to trust that you have truly been forgiven. When you have harmed someone and have repented of the wrong you have done; when you ache with regret and beg for their pardon; when you long for things to be again as they were before your offense, but suspect that they can never be so; then part of you despairs that full forgiveness can in reality ever be given to you.

> When you deal intimately with human beings . . . you wonder at times if forgiveness is not as rare as hen's teeth. People bury hatchets but carefully tuck away the map which tells where their hidden weapon lies. We put our resentments in cold storage and then pull the switch to let them thaw out again. Our grudges are taken out to the lake to drown them—even the lake of prayer—and we end up giving them a swimming lesson. How often we have torn up the canceled note but hang on to the wastebasket that holds the pieces. This is not to say that human forgiveness does not occur; only that it is rare and that much that passes for forgiveness is often not so at all.[5]

As unfamiliar or uneasy as we may be with forgiveness, we are certainly well acquainted with disappointment; it is basic to our emotional pain when others hurt or fail us. The Bible that so confidently proclaims the miracle of forgiveness also unhesitatingly faces up to the realities of disappointment. The Scripture is utterly familiar with and sympathetic to the experiences that make it hard for us to be forgiving, recording faithfully the complaints of persons shocked, amazed, or saddened by the pain of injustice.

Job only needs to hear the theologically correct but accusing speech of one of his friends to begin to feel abandoned and to complain, "A despairing man should have the devotion of his friends . . . but my brothers are as undependable as intermittent streams . . . (where) caravans . . . look for water . . . only to be disappointed" (Job 6:14–20).

David, suffering the malice of his enemies, finds it most bitter that "Even my close friend, whom I trusted, he who shared my bread, has lifted up his heel against me" (Ps. 41:9).

And even Jesus who "knew what was in man," seems to speak in tones of disappointment when disciples desert, "You do not want to leave too, do you?" (John 6:67) and the closest of his friends fail at his most vulnerable moment, "Could you men not keep watch with me for one hour?" (Matt. 26:38–40).

The Promise of Forgiveness

In the face of such persistent honesty about the pervasive experience of being victimized and disappointed, the Scripture, nevertheless, exuberantly proclaims the importance and wonders of forgiveness, both as it is offered to us and as we are enabled to offer it to others. Let us consider two examples.

Some Bible interpreters have commented that the first book of the Bible closes with words which ironically mark the predicament of humankind because of the fall into sin and its penalty, death: "... in a coffin in Egypt" (Gen. 50:26). But that final page of the Bible's opening document also records an incident that poignantly prepares us for the answer of God to our sin and death, the answer that is central to Scripture and crucial to redeemed human relationships: forgiveness.[6]

> When Joseph's brothers saw that their father was dead, they said, "What if Joseph holds a grudge against us and pays us back for all the wrongs we did to him?" So they sent word to Joseph, saying, "Your father left these instructions before he died: 'This is what you are to say to Joseph: I ask you to forgive your brothers the sins and the wrongs they committed in treating you so badly.' Now please forgive the sins of the servants of the God of your father." When their message came to him, Joseph wept.
>
> His brothers then came and threw themselves down before him. "We are your slaves," they said. But Joseph said to them, "Don't be afraid. Am I in the place of God? You intended to harm me, but God intended it for good to accomplish what is now being done, the saving of many lives. So then, don't be afraid. I will provide for you, and your children." And he reassured them and spoke kindly to them.
>
> Genesis 50:15–21

In Joseph's encounter with his brothers we discover several elements in the importance and power of forgiveness. To begin with, Joseph does not belittle the heinousness of his brothers' actions. Forgiveness takes brokenness seriously and affirms that guilt is real, but also affirms that guilt is not the last word. While agreeing with his brothers' confession of responsibility for his suffering, Joseph opens the way to new beginnings in their relationships with

him (vv. 20–21, "you intended to harm me, but . . . don't be afraid").
Again, we should observe that Joseph seems to see through and
beyond his brothers' clumsy attempt to manipulate his sympathy
with a fictitious message in their father's name (vv. 16–17) and
understand some of their feelings of fear and mistrust. Certainly
his weeping (v. 17) is because at last they admit their wrong and
ask his forgiveness, but also because he is now able to relinquish
both the roles of victim and of judge (v. 19, "Am I in the place of
God?") and see himself as more like than unlike the persons who
have hurt him. That ability is evidence of Joseph's own progress in
healing from the emotional wounds suffered in his brothers' cruelties. With God's help he has been "rewriting" his memories and
realizing that his recall of painful events is not the whole picture
of his life. He sees God's providence even in his brothers' malice
and is able to think beyond the consequences for himself and be
glad that his suffering led to "the saving of many lives" (v. 20).
Joseph is now willing to leave the past alone and turn away from
wounded retribution. He may not be able to resolve in his thinking
all the reasons for the pain that overtook him, but he can accept
the ambiguity, see the overcoming hand of God, and be free of
bondage to the past. Lyman Lundeen observes, "In this way, forgiveness gives freedom from the past and from its pain. Something
more promising captures our attention."[7]

Joseph's brothers show a common misunderstanding of the
nature of forgiveness as they attempt to negotiate a new standing
with Joseph (v. 18, "We are your slaves"). This may be partly a cul-
turally conventional way of speaking to one in the high position of
power now enjoyed by their brother, but certainly both Joseph and
the brothers are aware that he is, in fact, exactly in position to make
his mercy to them part of a contract whereby they pay for their
guilt with some form of bondage.

But forgiveness shuns such "contracts," in favor of the boundless
possibilities it hopes for in the vitality of grace. "Wherever life with
others is dominated by a 'contract' arrangement, both the individual and the individual's relationships with others are diminished."[8]
Joseph will not consider having such power over his brothers; he
opts rather for the power of free forgiveness enabled by his God.

Contractual kinds of agreements about behavior between the

perpetrator and the victim can fashion a kind of fairness and "just deserts" solution to broken relationships, but it is an impersonal solution that heals superficially. So far does the power of forgiveness take Joseph beyond the need of such manipulated control that he is able to give blessing instead of exacting tribute! (Verse 21, "So then, don't be afraid, I will provide for you and your children.") In the Hebrew, the "I" is emphatic, telling us that Joseph is promising something more than official philanthropy; he is determined to be personally involved in the lives of their families for ongoing good and filial caring. As Lundeen observes, "Forgiveness is an initiative that liberates individuals without the loss of relationships. It asserts openness in the face of the momentum of past decisions; instead of isolating victims and oppressors, it opens the way to new beginnings . . . In the end, the kind of liberation forgiveness offers ties us together rather than separates us . . . Forgiveness changes the entire situation for individuals. It frees them to be themselves— together . . . Forgiveness can sustain the drive for greater fairness, but it does so by going beyond it."[9]

Finally, we see that Joseph's forgiveness is very much grounded in his faith in God's living presence. Just how real God and his grace are to the brothers may be hard to discern with certainty. Their appeal to common faith and covenantal solidarity (v. 17, "Now please forgive the sins of the servants of the God of your father") may be suspected as yet another manipulative strategy. But the vital factor in this story of the importance of forgiveness is that Joseph at least clearly links God's grace to his own reasons for forgiving (vv. 19–20). Thus we are confronted with the marvel of the hard-work miracle! Those we forgive may be neither adequately repentant nor ready to be honest with us in all parts of our future relationship, but by the grace of God genuine forgiveness can still be freely given so we, like Joseph, learn to trust the active presence of God in our own lives and believe its possibilities in theirs.

Lundeen affirms this, "Forgiveness opens space for a personal God who takes free, restoring initiatives. God as the ground and goal of all human endeavor is not some rigid reality that we simply bump up against. God is not a kind of impersonal lawmaker or an objective judge who stands at a distance from human affairs. Stressing forgiveness makes God, as ultimate context, a personal and caring reality in whom human life has place and meaning . . . If the dynamics of forgiveness on a human level prompts us to look to God, the whole history of God in Christ presses toward center stage. In Christ forgiveness is made clear. The deep personal dimensions of freedom in relationships surface. God is seen as the lover who suffers for the guilty in such a dependable and decisive way that we can build all our hope around him."[10]

With this affirmation pointing us to Jesus Christ, let us find a second biblical example of the importance of forgiveness in the words of our Savior himself:

> Jesus said to his disciples: "Things that cause people to sin are bound to come, but woe to that person through whom they come. It would be better for him to be thrown into the sea with a millstone tied around his neck than for him to cause one of these little ones to sin. So watch yourselves. If your brother sins, rebuke him, and if he repents, forgive him. If he sins against you seven times in a day, and seven times comes back to you and says, 'I repent,' forgive him." The apostles said to the Lord, "Increase our faith!" He replied, "If you have faith as small as a mustard seed, you can say to this mulberry tree, 'Be uprooted and planted in the sea,' and it will obey you. Suppose one of you had a servant plowing or looking after the sheep. Would he say to the servant when he comes in from the field, 'Come along now and sit down to eat?' Would he not rather say, 'Prepare my supper, get yourself ready and wait on me while I eat and drink; after that you may eat and drink'? Would he thank the servant because he did what he was told to do? So you also, when you have done everything you were told to do, should say, 'We are unworthy servants; we have only done our duty.'"
>
> Luke 17:1–10

Jesus begins his remarks to his disciples with the realism we have come to expect from our incarnate Lord; realism about the frequency and seriousness of sin; about our own susceptibility and the step-by-patient-step nature of forgiveness.

The glory of the miracle that is forgiveness blazes forth against the darkly somber picture Jesus gives his disciples of the stern judgment due to those who cause others to sin. Better to die a violent death than to be responsible for the temptation of a vulnerable brother or sister! (vv. 1–3a). In light of this fearful condemnation of the kind of betrayal of trusting human relationships of which we all are capable, how welcome and wondrous is the possibility of forgiveness!

The hard work that is forgiveness is the next topic of Jesus' teaching: Forgiveness is a process involving repeated condescension to the failures of the one who has offended you. ("Seven times a day" means there is no end to the responsibility to forgive. Compare Jesus' expansion on this principle in Matthew 18:21–22, "seventy times seven".) The disciples are overwhelmed by the difficulty of such a standard of behavior. How much faith are we going to need to be *that* forgiving? To take risks with people like *that*? To be *that* vulnerable to further hurt? Jesus' reply to their astonished query is that it isn't really a matter at all of how much more faith they will need; a little faith is potentially powerful beyond ordinary expectations! (v. 6). It is really a matter of obedient effort growing out of an understanding of our own humanness and the servant-Lord nature of our commitment to God.

Once again, as we saw in Joseph's life, ability to forgive involves my reinterpreting my position as victim: Am I really superior to the culprit who injured me? Are we not more alike than unlike? This recognition does not excuse their action or their responsibility to repent (v. 3, " . . . rebuke him, and if he repents. . . ."), but it is a vital step toward becoming ready to forgive and it does not involve some esoteric level of spirituality. Forgiveness is not only for the spiritually advanced!

Using a typical day in the life of a household servant, Jesus next tells a parable to illustrate this principle in forgiving someone who has hurt you, even repeatedly. The parable is keenly realistic; the servant's task was against personal feelings and comfort, very hard at the moment and apparently thankless. (Jesus does not condone slavery, but simply uses a slice of life in current society to make his point. On another occasion in Luke 12:35–37, he tells a parable in which the master reverses the normal roles and humbly serves his servants. That story symbolizes God's grace to us, this one symbolizes our proper servant attitude toward one another.) The disciples' need in forgiving was not more faith, but to use the faith which they already had and obey God's will that they forgive. Forgiveness is not initially a feeling; it is chosen actions, by which, even before you can feel forgiving, you carry out forgiveness by not using past (six failures already today!) offenses against the offender. You can at least take beginning steps, even if you have to put it in terms of only doing your duty (v. 10) and finding a way to begin the work of the forgiveness process.

In both of these scriptural examples we are impressed by the crucial importance of forgiveness. For Joseph it meant being released from bondage to the past by forgiving the almost unforgivable cruelties of his brothers. For Jesus' disciples it meant that the peril of condemnation for sin in relationships is matched by the miracle of forgiving grace, but that the miracle is one to be repeated in our own choices toward those who sin against us.

The power of forgiveness is incalculable, its place in healing emotional wounds is crucial, and it is a miracle repeated beyond the pages of Scripture in the lives of God's people today. This is evident in the story of one Christian couple who are representative of so many. Herb and Margaret struggled to keep their marriage together in the face of Herb's history of homosexual activity and severe depression rooted in experiences of childhood abuse and unforgiving parental perfectionism. The key to their continuing to win the struggle was Margaret's persistent example of forgiveness.

Herb would ask again and again, "Why do you stay and put up with me? Why haven't you taken the kids and left?", and repeatedly, though her pain was great and her endurance tested severely, Margaret would affirm her love for him and her belief that things would be better someday. Herb couldn't see how Margaret could still love him. And how could she ever forgive him when he couldn't forgive himself? He stated that even after he finally gave up homosexual activities, he felt unforgivable. "I knew that was a big part of my problem. So did my therapist. Though she never claimed to be a Christian she once chided me, saying, 'I don't understand. The basis of your Christian faith is a God who forgives all your sins, and yet you can't forgive yourself.'"

Later Herb could state that part of his problem was that he couldn't believe God would forgive him for the things he had done. He knew what the Bible said about a heavenly Father's forgiveness. But he couldn't reconcile that in his human mind, or with his human experience. He said, "I read books on the subject. But nothing explained how God could forgive sins and remember them no more as the Bible claimed. How could an all-knowing God really forget?"

If it hadn't been for Margaret's patient example of human forgiveness, Herb never would have been able to believe in God's forgiveness. But he finally did, after years of struggle. And whenever he began to doubt it, Margaret would gently remind him that God had indeed forgiven him of everything.[11]

2

The Possibility
of Forgiveness

In his book, *Being Holy, Being Human*, Jay Kesler quotes Eric Webster, "Handling people need not be so difficult—all you need is inexhaustible patience, unfailing insight, unshakable nervous stability, an unbreakable will, decisive judgment, infrangible physique, irrepressible spirits, plus unfeigned affection for all people—and an awful lot of experience."[1] The rest of us who cannot live up to these qualifications are going to rejoice in the unfailing help of our Lord who meets the special needs of his imperfect servants.

Where will we find the ability to forgive, to receive forgiveness, and as often discouraged ministers of the gospel, to teach and counsel—and model—forgiveness? The answer of the Scripture is that we shall find such help in God himself and in the powers that are imparted by the grace he gives to us.

The possibility of forgiveness is rooted in the character and actions of God. If we lived in a universe created and governed by anyone other than the Christian God, there would be no hope of forgiveness. The forgiveness of our own sins, our forgiveness of the sins of others against us, and our forgiveness of ourselves for our own sins are all made possible by who God is and what he has done.

As with the other graces of the Christian life, the origin of forgiveness lies first and foremost in the character of God himself. This, then, must be our starting point in considering the possibility of our giving and receiving forgiveness.

God's Forgiveness Is Rooted in His Eternal Character

In the midst of the worst crisis of his troubled leadership of Israel, the judgment of the people for their worship of the golden calf, Moses, fearful of losing God's presence, prays to see God's glory (Exod. 32–34). In response, God reveals himself by proclaiming his name, "the Lord," and the moral character that name encompasses.

> Then the LORD came down in the cloud and stood there with him and proclaimed his name, the LORD. And he passed in front of Moses, proclaiming, "The LORD, the LORD, the compassionate and gracious God, slow to anger, abounding in love and faithfulness, maintaining love to thousands, and forgiving wickedness, rebellion and sin. Yet he does not leave the guilty unpunished. . . ."
>
> Exodus 34:5–7

In this disclosure, echoed in later Scriptures (e.g., Neh. 9:17; Ps. 86:15; Joel 2:13), God shows that forgiveness is foundational to his nature. As we shall consider later, he also shows that forgiveness is not incompatible with realism about the guilt of human sin.

When did God begin to be a forgiving God? At the cross? In the exodus? When he pronounced judgment upon Satan with the first promise of a Savior for fallen humankind? (Gen. 3:15). Scripture compels us to deduce that forgiveness is part of God's *eternal* character! It was God's nature before it was needed!

- "This grace was given us in Christ Jesus before the beginning of time. . . ."(2 Tim. 1:9).
- "He chose us in him before the creation of the world to be holy and blameless in his sight" (Eph. 1:4).

If the incomparable and timeless mystery of God's eternal plan for our salvation existed before sin, then the heart of God was a forgiving heart before human hearts chose evil! We cannot explain it, but like the apostles who put this truth into the context of thanksgiving (1 Thess. 1:4–6; 2:13; 1 Peter 1:20–21), we can only praise the God who is the source of such blessing.

God's Forgiveness Is Incomparable

The hope of our ever being able to forgive others is grounded in the incomparably wondrous nature of God's own forgiveness. Our hope lies in the fact that God's forgiveness is immeasurably superior to ours. This should not be cause for despair but for rejoicing.

> God's forgiveness cannot be understood by analyzing the nature of human forgiveness. When Israel was invited to salvation in the way of repentance, the promise of comfort was added that God would have mercy and abundantly pardon (Isa. 55:6–7). But it was also stated that "My thoughts are not your thoughts, neither are your ways my ways," declares the Lord. "As the heavens are higher than the earth, so are my ways higher than your ways and my thoughts than your thoughts" (55:8–9). Therefore, the divine forgiveness could only be heard and accepted as the content of a truly new and astonishing *tidings of salvation*. . . . God, we read, shall "tread our iniquities under foot" and "cast all our sins into the depths of the sea" (Micah 7:19); he shall sweep them away as a cloud and mist (Isa. 44:22) and cast them behind his back (38:17). In all of this, as Israel's God, he cannot be *compared*. "Who is a God like thee, pardoning iniquity . . . ?"[2]

In this fact there should be great comfort for us because God's forgiveness is presented to us in the Bible as incomparably available and enduring. What hope we are given that our sins can never exhaust God's mercy!

But help in making forgiveness possible comes to us from God in the form of yet another truth about his nature.

God's Forgiveness Is Coupled with His Realism about Sin

We must not construe from God's forgiving nature that he is, therefore, indifferent to sin. When, for example, in the process of dealing with our emotional wounds we undertake to reexperience the pain suffered at the hands of another person, we need to understand that we have God's example when we refuse to ignore the reality of the wrong done to us. God's forgiveness of sin is certainly not an overlooking of the gravity of the offense. God does not easily forgive because he was never really angry. Our anger at those who hurt us is at least in this way like God's anger—it is real. God never avoids the true nature of our evil human behavior.

- "... forgiving wickedness, rebellion, and sin. Yet he does not leave the guilty unpunished. . . ." (Exod. 34:7).
- "Woe to those who call evil good and good evil, who put darkness for light and light for darkness, who put bitter for sweet and sweet for bitter" (Isa. 5:20).
- "If we claim to be without sin, we deceive ourselves and the truth is not in us. If we confess our sins, he is faithful and just and will forgive us our sins and purify us from all unrighteousness. If we claim we have not sinned, we make him out to be a liar and his word has no place in our lives" (1 John 1:8–10).

One of the clearest truths in the biblical message is that God's forgiveness is not set in the context of watering down or relativizing human sin. To the contrary, God is revealed to be truly and consistently angry with sin.

"Divine forgiveness is never in Scripture an indifferent love or a matter of God's *being blind*. It is rather a turning from real *wrath* to real *grace* . . . the Bible's message (is) of jubilee and forgiveness—a message tied together in a single package with the knowledge of the wrath of God against man's sin."[3]

This realistic anger of God against evil is consistently seen in the life and ministry of Jesus. Significantly it is Jesus, the "Lamb of God who takes away the sin of the world" (John 1:29), who is "led like a lamb to the slaughter" with the "iniquity of us all" upon his innocent soul. It is this same Jesus who suffers for us in silent submission (Isa. 53:6–7), but who is said to be unswervingly wrathful with sin. In judgment the wicked cry out to be hidden from "the face of him who sits on the throne and from the *wrath of the Lamb*"!

So we find that God's forgiveness is a miracle, accomplished without overlooking the reality and destructiveness of human sin for a moment. It is against the dark backdrop of real evil that God reveals his grace in its impact on the guilty human heart.

- "For his anger lasts only a moment, but his favor lasts a lifetime. Weeping may remain for a night, but rejoicing comes in the morning" (Ps. 30:5).
- "I will heal their waywardness and love them freely, for my anger has turned away from them" (Hos. 14:4).

This brings us to another unique factor in the forgiveness that comes from the Lord himself.

God's Forgiveness Is Embraced in His Justice

We know that the key question of the New Testament, indeed of the whole Bible, is "How can God be just and yet be the justifier of sinners?" How can God be truly angry at sin, truly punish sin, yet truly forgive a sinner and continue to be holy and just?

Here the gospel points to the cross as the focus of God's justice. It is precisely there, where the Son of God suffers the anger of God in our place, that the gospel shows us how seriously God takes sin and how justly he accomplishes forgiving grace. Sin *is* paid for; sin *is* justly punished. At the cross God's mercy and grace cut through the problem of just punishment for our sins. But it is not fair! It is not fair for Jesus to suffer for the guilty—for my guilt! No, it is not, but here, here in this Great Unfairness lies the power that not only makes it possible for God to forgive me, but also for me to learn to forgive those who hurt me! What we learn from God's forgiveness of us is that forgiveness does not have anything to do with fairness. Forgiveness cuts through the whole question of just deserts.

The heart of the possibility of forgiveness is that God forgives because his justice has been satisfied, satisfied by the atonement provided by his love in giving his only Son for us. As "unfair" as that solution is, it is an unfairness absorbed into the heart of God by his merciful acceptance of the unfairness!

The Doctrine of Divine Satisfaction

The doctrine of divine satisfaction is the biblical teaching that Christ, by offering his sinless life in our place, bore the full, rightful punishment for our sin, suffering all that the law of God required of sinners and, therefore, satisfied God's justice forever and set us free from all obligation to atone for our own sins.

> The atonement is rooted in the love and justice of God; love offered sinners a way of escape, and justice demanded that the requirements of the law should be met (John 3:16; Rom. 3:24–26). The atonement . . . served to render satisfaction to God . . . Christ . . . atoned for the sin of mankind by bearing the penalty of sin and meeting the demands of the law, and thus wrought an eternal redemption for man . . . The offended party himself made provision for the atonement . . .[4]

What has this doctrine to do with our ability to forgive those who hurt us? Just this: By the power of the Holy Spirit we may share in God's satisfaction even if we receive little or no satisfaction within our human relationship with the one who hurt us. This is the great psychological implication of the theology of divine satisfaction.

When I have been wronged, I may feel I can only forgive if certain requirements are met. For example, I may judge that I can only be satisfied if the wrong is acknowledged, the wrong is punished, and that which was wrongly taken from me can be restored. Let us consider each of these in turn.

I may feel that the wrong must be acknowledged. In the best scenario, the one who sinned against me will come to see the wrong and confess it to me. But suppose he or she does not acknowledge that the wrong was done?

While the one who hurt me may not acknowledge the wrong, God my heavenly Father does. Thus, the only one who can fully and accurately assess the nature of the crime, agrees with me that I have indeed been wronged. The only one (God) able to realize the true depth of my pain faces the realities of that suffering with me. (Isa. 63:9, "In all their distress he too was distressed. . . .") Can I be satisfied with that?

I may feel that the wrong must be punished. In the best of situations, guilty persons are convicted and pay the appropriate penalty for their offenses. But suppose the one who has hurt me is never brought to task for their deeds done to me? The culprit may not be punished, but Christ my Savior was. Just as he died for the sins I have committed, so he also died for the sins committed against me. Justice is done in the highest court! I think I would be satisfied if my tormentor, a finite creature, was made to pay the price for the wrong done to me. But the price actually paid was so much more costly, even the infinite life of the Son of God! Can I be satisfied with that?

I may feel that what was wrongly taken from me must be restored. But it rarely can be. Not often can the culprit give back what he or she has "stolen." A childhood spoiled by abuse, marriage broken by unfaithfulness, friendship shattered by betrayal; too much is lost that cannot be replaced—it is lost in irretrievable time. The perpetrator may not be willing or able to compensate for what cannot be undone.

But God promises to do so! Ultimately in heaven, and partly now in the healing fellowship of the body of Christ, God will restore all that is lost.

God satisfied his Son for his suffering ("After the suffering of his soul, he will see the light of life, and be satisfied. . . ." Isa. 53:11) and God will satisfy us for ours. ("And I—in righteousness I will see your face; when I awake, I will be satisfied with seeing your likeness," Ps. 17:15.)

Can I now be satisfied with God's promise of satisfaction? Can I live without compensation from those who hurt me and can I, through trust in God, find grace to forgive the culprit? All these things are possible because of what God has done and who he is.

How can I rise to this level of being satisfied, of letting God's satisfaction be mine? The Father is satisfied with the sacrifice of the Son; the Son is satisfied by the resurrection and exaltation given him by the Father; now the Scripture seems to indicate that the Holy Spirit can impact the results of that divine satisfaction to me. The satisfied mind of Christ is given to us and we are instructed that we can experience the attitudes of his mind ("We have the mind of Christ," 1 Cor. 2:16; "Your attitude should be the same as that of Christ Jesus," Phil. 2:5).

This mind is created in you with the new life impacted by the Spirit when he brings you out of death into life; when he makes you begin to be a new creation (2 Cor. 5:17); when he begins the "renewing of your mind" that transforms your thinking (Rom. 12:2) about life's choices and the people in your world.

> We cannot sacrifice enough to heal the one who hurts us. We are not able to forgive equal to our spouses sinning—nor when such giving must come solely from ourselves. But if forgiveness is a tool, it is also a power tool whose power comes from a source other than ourselves. We may use it; we may carefully and self-consciously apply it to our spouses; but Jesus Christ empowers it. He is the true source of its transfiguring love. And the love of the Son of God is infinite.[5]

Walter Wangerin Jr. makes this statement out of his own experience of being forgiven by his wife, Thanne, for offending her tender spirit. Listen to their experience. It illustrates well how the mind that shares this satisfaction of God can be enabled to forgive beyond human possibility:

> Thanne could not forgive me. This is a plain fact. My sin was greater than her capacity to forgive, had lasted longer than her kindness, had grown more oppressive than her goodness. This was not a single act nor a series of acts, but my being. My sin was the murder of her spirit, the unholy violation of her sole identity—the blithe assumption of her presence, as though she were furniture. I had broken her. How could a broken person be at the same time whole enough to forgive? No: Thanne was created finite, and could not forgive me.
>
> But Jesus could.
>
> One day Thanne stood in the doorway of my study, looking at me. I turned in my chair and saw that she was not angry. Small Thanne, delicate, diminutive Thanne, she was not glaring, but gazing at me with gentle, questioning eyes. This was totally unexpected, both her presence and her expression. There was no reason why she should be standing there, no detail I've forgotten to tell you. Yet, for a full minute we looked at one another; and then she walked to my side where I sat. She touched my shoulder. She said, "Wally, will you hug me?"

I leaped from my chair, I wrapped her all around in two arms and squeezed my wife, my wife, so deeply in my body—and we both burst into tears.

Would I hug her? Oh, but the better question was, would she let me hug her? And she did. Dear Lord Jesus, where did this come from, this sudden, unnatural, undeserved willingness to let me touch her, hug her, love her? Not from me! I was her ruination. Not from her, because I had killed that part of her. From you!

How often had we hugged before? I couldn't count the times. How good had those hugs been? I couldn't measure the goodness. But this hug—don't you know, it was my salvation, different from any other and more remarkable because this is the hug I should never have had. That is forgiveness! The law was gone. Rights were all abandoned. Mercy took their place. We were married again. And it was you, Christ Jesus, in my arms—within my graceful Thanne. One single, common hug, and we were alive again.

Thanne gave me a gift: She gave me the small plastic figure of a woman with her eyes rolled up, her mouth skewed to one side, the tongue lolling out, a cartoon face. I have this gift in my study today. The inscription at the bottom reads: "I love you so much it hurts."[6]

Indeed the work of forgiving love can hurt. For the Wangerins this was a powerful beginning in the experience of the miracle of forgiveness; but hard work was to follow as they pursued the practice of forgiving and sought to preserve its accomplishments. So let us now consider some matters which can make the hard work more endurable.

Increasing the Possibility of Forgiving

This possibility that I may be able to forgive one who has hurt me will be greatly increased when I remember some things that forgiving is not.

Forgiving is not forgetting. To quickly forget a hurt is to repress it and repression does not lead to genuine healing. The emotional pain, the sting of memory, and my preoccupation with the wrong done to me may fade with time and have less and less emotional energy attached to them. But forgiveness does not eliminate memory. What it does is enable us to control memory, to begin to remember without malice. Rebuilding a relationship may involve creating new, better memories together, but that is different from desperate attempts to "kiss-and-make-up," to hide bad memories under a cover-up of frantically contrived new experiences, new location, or new possessions.

Forgiving is not excusing. Part of the healing of emotional wounds is reinterpreting the hurt which includes seeing the one who hurt me as more like than unlike me.

> I may have never hurt another by sexually abusing a young child, or by destroying the character of someone by means of slander and lies, or by violating a marriage through adultery. But I am capable of any and all of these acts. And until I can recognize that "there, but for the grace of God, go I," I am incapable of experiencing full and complete healing of the depths of my hurts. When I can allow myself to identify with those who hurt me by seeing myself to be made of the same basic fabric, then, and only then, will I be able to understand my reaction to them and fully release the anger. Only then will forgiveness be something other than an act of condescension which is never a satisfactory basis for a genuine release of anger.[7]

But such understanding that I share my abuser's humanness is not the same as excusing the behavior of this one who hurt me. There are always reasons why other people behave as they do and sometimes these reasons will even make sense to us if we come to know them. However, reasons and shared human weakness are not the same as excuses.

Excuses tend to gloss over the reality of evil, of personal responsibility for wrongs done to another. Indeed, explaining away responsibility for bad behavior is the growing mind-set in our society.

Professor Roger Lundin of Wheaton College tells of the student responses to an essay question on a test he gave. "It asked students to describe the consequences of the fall as John Milton depicts them in Book IX of *Paradise Lost*. Most answers focused upon the discord that entered Adam and Eve's relationship, their shame, and their drastically altered view of God. But several exams contained surprising responses. Each began with a thesis statement something like this: 'The major effect of the fall was to make Adam and Eve change their lifestyle.' What has concerned me over the years has been the inability of many students, when I have related this story to them, to understand the dangers inherent in reducing the expulsion from Eden to a change in lifestyle. A world in which every action manifests nothing more than an individual's flair, his or her peculiar 'style,' is a world in which there is no difference in choosing between gods to worship and ice cream flavors to consume."[8]

If the consequences of wrongs done to us or by us are allowed to become merely problems of lifestyle and the cause of each wrong blamed upon peer pressure or a history of victimization by others, then there is no need for forgiveness because all deeds are excusable.

In fact, most of what we do to one another in the conflicts of human relationships are inexcusable. Attempts to excuse will block efforts to genuinely forgive and can often turn to bitterness when memory eventually becomes more honest.

Forgiving is not ignoring. I may attempt to ignore the feelings of hurt, or even the person who hurt me, pretending it did not happen or minimizing it in my thinking. A form of this may be my assumption that "time heals all wounds" and try to be patient until my pain goes away or until the one who wounded me acknowledges the wrong, repents, and approaches me with offered restitution. But to ignore or overlook wrong is an attempt to change reality by the power of selective memory and will not produce genuine healing.

Forgiving is not necessarily to offer unconditional trust. In some circumstances I may discern the other person's remorse to be genuine enough to produce changed behavior, and, therefore, conclude that I can safely extend complete trust without guarding myself further against recurring hurt. However, in other situations caution is called for, and I must not assume that I will never again be hurt in the same way by the same person. I should then take steps to minimize that possibility. I may genuinely forgive the past and at the same time be cautious around the one who hurt me. Forgiveness is not always incompatible with limited trust.

These are common misunderstandings about the real nature of the forgiving process. Forgiveness is hard enough work that one does not want to assume the fruitless burden of impossible and disappointing tasks! Actually the prospect of forgiving is lightened considerably by avoiding these misunderstandings.

Experiencing the Possibility of Forgiving

In succeeding chapters we shall examine further the true nature of forgiveness, and some steps in *receiving forgiveness*. But at this point, let us briefly look at several steps which are effective *for the victim* in the forgiving process.

Along the way to accomplishing forgiveness you will need to:

Consider how you were forgiven. As I prepare to move toward a person with forgiveness, I must remember that I am not superior to this other sinner. I may never have committed his or her exact sin, but I am still more similar to them than to the righteous God! I, too, hurt others as I act out my own brokenness, need, and woundedness (or my own selfishness!).

I must take time to recall some of my own specific sins against others, against friends, spouse, parents, and colleagues. I must remember, even if long ago committed and repented of, some of my offenses or acts of neglect against the poor, people of another class or race, or carelessly against strangers. I must think, too, about how I have committed in imagination or desire what I have not done in reality.

All this I should do, not to put myself back under the oppression of guilt over previously forgiven sins, but to feel again a sense of rejoicing gratitude for God's mercy to me and to prepare to forgive "as God in Christ has forgiven me."

Be realistic. The steps in forgiving may be accomplished successfully only if I proceed realistically in two ways: name the sin against me for what it truly is; and limit my expectations of what will result from forgiveness.

In naming the offense I have suffered, I must neither belittle it nor exaggerate it.

M. Scott Peck tells us of the need to face the reality of our hurt as he discusses evil in one's own family. "To come to terms with evil in one's parentage is perhaps the most difficult and painful psychological task a human being can be called on to face. Most fail and become its victims. Those who fully succeed in developing the necessary searing vision are those who are able to name it. For to 'come to terms' means to 'arrive at the name.' As therapists, it is our duty to do what is in our power to assist evil's victims to arrive at the true name of their affliction."[9]

Such honest exploration of the past may give great pain but it may also bring some true comfort.

> The monsters we fear in the dark closets of our unconscious mind always shrink in size when we turn the light of truth upon them. This is the heart of the psychoanalytic view of the therapeutic nature of insight. As understood in psychoanalysis, insight could be described as a knowledge of our own conscious and unconscious feelings and thoughts that constructively alter our perception of ourselves and of others, bringing both into greater conformity with reality. Therapeutic insight does not merely refer to the acquisition of some piece of information about myself. It is a connection between my inner and outer worlds, between my past and my present, between my unconscious and my conscious states of mind. And genuine insight, as opposed to mere knowledge, always promotes healing and growth.[10]

The intellectual activity that is necessary for healing is that which brings truth to bear on the situation. When we are suffering emotional damage from the wrongs done to us, our understanding can be distorted. For healing to occur, our perceptions must be brought in line with reality, the truth of what happened. Again, before attempting to forgive the one who hurt me, it is also important to have expectations about what will result from the act of forgiveness. First, I should be clear about the fact that forgiveness may not heal the relationship with the person who hurt me. That person may not admit fault, may not be ready to receive forgiveness from me, or may, in other ways, not be ready to change. I must seek to extend forgiveness without regard to these consequences, giving because I choose now to do so, not because I expect it to produce a hoped for response in the other. Such response would perhaps make me feel better about my adversary, but I cannot be bound by what they may or may not do. Likewise, I must not expect that my act of forgiving will immediately make me feel better within myself. I must not doubt the genuineness of my act of forgiveness if I still feel anger or hurt after I forgive the person who hurt me.

Finally, I must realize that forgiveness is seldom a one time affair. Usually I must forgive over and over again. (Remember our discussion of Luke 17:1–10 in chapter 1.) Each subsequent offering of forgiveness renders the former ones more complete, but usually it is only God who can forgive completely at once!

Share the pain. In facing the realistic truth and in accepting the burden of repeated forgiving steps, I may find myself reexperiencing the pain of the original hurt to such an extent that I need the aid of a counselor or at least the comfort of a sympathetic friend.

In a remarkable way, sharing an experience does make the load less heavy. To share an experience of pain with someone who is willing to listen empathically is to allow them to take our burden upon themselves and, thereby, share it with us. And in sharing, our load is lightened and we are strengthened. (Gal. 6:2, "Carry each other's burdens. . . .")

Christ himself is described as bearing our burdens, carrying our sorrows, taking upon himself our sickness and infirmities, and thereby healing us (Isa. 53:4; Matt. 8:17). Thus, when we feel ourselves overwhelmed by our hurts, disappointments, losses, or the reawakening of past pain, we should remember that Jesus is always available to share these burdens with us.

But sharing experiences with the Lord should not replace sharing them when possible with other humans. Sometimes sharing feelings with God is a way to prepare for sharing them with others. At other times, problems seem more readily shared with other humans, and God's love, in these situations, is communicated to us through the love of another person.

Accept the time forgiving may take. We have already observed that forgiveness is not a shock treatment that instantly wipes out our memory of the offenses we have suffered. And we have acknowledged that it's not a single dose medication that need not be repeated. In addition, we need to realize and absorb the reality that forgiving, especially forgiving greater hurts, may be a pilgrimage of years, perhaps a lifetime journey. Some conflicts may only be healed completely by the resurrection of the last day! But God wants us to seek to begin healing now, inasmuch as we are in his eyes already raised from death to life spiritually and continual recipients of his enabling grace and power.

Understand what it means to "forgive and forget." God tells us that having forgiven us, he "remembers" our sins "no more" (Jer. 31:34; Heb. 8:12; 10:17). Since we are to forgive as we have been forgiven, is it then expected of us to literally forget the hurts done to us? The answer to this is found in the kind of "forgetting" exercised by God himself. He is omniscient, knowing all things possible at all times and at every moment in time. God cannot forget our sins in the sense that he loses them from his memory. By forgetting then, he must mean that he sets aside the punishment we deserve when he forgives us. He holds the guilt of our sins over our heads no longer. Our past culpability is not a factor in how he treats us in the future—except to continue his forgiving, healing mercy. So when we "forget" the offenses done to us, it means we will not in the future "use" the offense as reason to punish the offender. We will not raise it as an issue between us; not use it as a weapon in arguments. We will not continually remind third parties about it. And we will determine to work at not dwelling upon it in our own minds. This is what it means "to forgive and forget."

Finally, learn ways to break the chain of self-enslavement to bitter thoughts. Brooding over the past allows that which is gone, and exists no longer except in my mind, to make me miserable today. Self-pity leads to anger, anger may lead to bitterness and then to depression. Keep in mind that the following may be far too simple for handling the memory of the monstrous offenses we may suffer, but it may prove helpful in the more common interpersonal pains. Break the chain of brooding at its earliest link by:

1. Whenever you begin to recall your loss, take two minutes to think about it (time yourself). The fact of the offense is a sad one and the loss to your peace is real, but you cannot allow yourself to be immobilized by it. Forgiveness can give you more and more control over memory. You are free to recall the hurt if you choose and also free to not entertain thoughts of it if it comes into your consciousness.
2. Conclude the two-minute period in prayer to God, place your hurt in his hands, and ask for help to put it behind you. Ask for the freedom Jesus promises to give (John 8:36).

3. Get up and turn to a present chore or responsibility and pour your energies productively into it. Or, if this is a period for leisure, concentrate on your enjoyment! Best of all, turn to the Scriptures, find a passage which presents God in his majesty (often this will be a psalm) and focus on how that portion and the beauty of his attributes have a way of shrinking our own loss down to size. (Remember the "think about these things" passage in Philippians 4:8–9. God himself is "noble," "right," "pure," "lovely," and "admirable." And he is the "God of peace" who "will be with you.")

3

The Necessity
of Forgiveness

A strange story entitled "Cold Storage" was published by neurologist Dr. Oliver Sacks in the British quarterly *Granta,* and reported in the *New Yorker Magazine.*[1] In it Dr. Sacks described a patient, identified as Uncle Toby, whom he met in 1957 in London. While making a house call to see a sick child, another doctor saw Uncle Toby sitting silent and motionless in a corner of a room. When he asked about the figure, the family explained matter-of-factly, "That's Uncle Toby. He's hardly moved in seven years."

Uncle Toby's initial slowing down had been so gradual as to go almost unnoticed. Later, it became so profound that it was just accepted by the family. "He was fed and watered daily," Dr. Sacks reports. "He was really no trouble . . . Most people never noticed him, still, silent in the corner. He was not regarded as ill; he had just come to a stop." Uncle Toby, it turned out, was suffering from a thyroid malfunction, and his metabolic rate had been reduced to almost zero. His temperature, which had to be measured on a special thermometer, proved to be sixty-eight degrees Fahrenheit—thirty degrees below normal. He was, in Dr. Sacks' words, "alive, but not alive; in abeyance, in cold storage." Over a period of weeks, doctors administered progressively larger doses of thyroxine to Uncle Toby, and his temperature rose steadily; soon he was walking and talking. Within a month, Dr. Sacks says, Uncle Toby had "awakened."

Most of the rest of the case study details the remarkable situations of both Uncle Toby, for whom not a moment had passed during the previous seven years, and his doctors, who were trying to decide how they might best coax their patient toward a realization of his predicament. But then the case took a darkly ironic turn. The doctors discovered that Uncle Toby had a highly malignant, rapidly proliferating "oat-cell" carcinoma. They managed to find x-rays taken seven years earlier and discovered early signs, overlooked at the time, of the cancer he now had. Such cancers ordinarily kill within a few months, but "it seemed that his cancer, like the rest of him, had been arrested, in cold storage," Dr. Sacks writes. Once he was warmed up, the growth of cancer increased rapidly and he expired several days later.[2]

There is an emotional and spiritual principle illustrated by this story, for guilt unforgiven or anger unreleased by forgiving can ultimately only damage us. We can deny, repress, and put our anger into "cold storage," but it will only grow again sometime! Body, mind, and spirit are inevitably, even if slowly, poisoned by unforgiven sin or by anger and resentment. The Bible bears solemn witness to this. Consider, for example, David, who tried to avoid dealing with his guilt and tells us:

> When I kept silent, my bones wasted away through my groaning all day long. For day and night your hand was heavy upon me; my strength was sapped as in the heat of summer. Then I acknowledged my sin to you . . . and you forgave the guilt of my sin.
>
> Psalm 32:3–5

Experience affirms the Bible's witness and finds the bondage of the angry to be no less harmful than that of the guilty. Author Dennis Guernsey writes, "I have really hated only one person in my life. I mean hatred that is obsessive. Hatred you can't let go of. The experience of hatred is still vivid in my memory. What I remember most is the addictive nature of the hatred. I got to where I liked thinking about my feelings toward the person. I fantasized about what I wished would happen to him. The thoughts about the situation that provoked my hatred would not go away. I soon came to realize that the hatred was controlling me rather than me controlling it. I was hooked."[3]

We harbor grudges, often against ourselves, and the stress of that unresolved anger may well result in physical illness, as well as unhealed, wounded relationships. "Try a simple experiment on yourself. Make a fist and hold it tight. One minute of this is sufficient to bring discomfort. Consider what would happen if the fist were maintained in that state of tension during a period that extended into weeks, months, or even years. Obviously it would soon become a sick member of the body."[4]

You may hurt a person by not forgiving them and thus feel some satisfying sense of getting even, but almost without exception, the hurt you do to yourself may be even greater. After a while you may not feel the pain of the clenched resentment in your soul, but its self-inflicted paralysis will have its effect upon your whole life.

Understanding the way in which unresolved anger can paralyze and destroy us from within requires that we understand the role of anger in emotional wounds.

The Psychology of Emotional Wounds

The first response to the experience of emotional hurt is a sense of loss. It is common for this loss to be covered by anger so quickly that most people are unaware that it is a part of their response to hurt. Emotional wounds always leave us with some diminished sense of self. It may be a loss of self-esteem or possibly of our sense of self-competence or worth. I experience the violations of trust usually involved in being wounded by another as something having been taken away from me. Indeed the common, often tearful cry of the victim of some form of abuse is, "I find it almost impossible now to really trust anyone!"

The dominant feelings associated with this experience of loss are those of vulnerability and sadness. But another feeling that often accompanies hurt is a feeling of being alone, of being abandoned or isolated. These feelings give particularly clear evidence of how central loss is to the experience of hurt. The pain associated with the experience of abandonment by a loved one, particularly a person on whom one depends for one's very existence, is probably as intense as emotional pain gets. But even when the feeling of abandonment is not part of the experience of hurt, the sense of loss is. Failure to begin to follow the way of forgiveness will inevitably only increase this sense of loss in the unforgiving person.

The feelings of anger usually come quickly after being the victim of hurt. Anger may be a very constructive force when it mobilizes us to action in response to some injustice or evil. However, anger may also fail us by being only a distraction for our pain and turning into a preoccupation with retaliatory fantasies, or when it moves us to inappropriate expression, which hurts others, or to repression, which hurts us. Further, the expression of anger is often very subtle. It can appear in many different guises, each of which masks to some extent the actual core of anger: depression, suspicion, jealousy, impatience, cynicism, and passive-aggressive behavior. With one or more of these faces, anger shows itself to be a part of the experience of hurt and an ongoing consequence of refusal to begin the process of forgiving.[5]

Dan Allender shows the effect of omitting forgiveness from therapy for healing of emotional wounds. "I talked to a woman who has been immersed for years in a secular approach to boundary building. Her mother is an evil, hard, critical woman who would rather destroy her daughter than admit that her husband abused the girl. For years the daughter set appropriate boundaries and 'took care of herself.' She had more peace and ease, but little joy or gentleness of soul. She was supposedly learning to love herself, but in so doing she'd lost the legitimate, God-honoring thrill of giving herself fully to another. In order to keep her boundaries high, she had to continually reaffirm the necessity of protecting herself and harden her heart to the sadness of her mother's life. She was transformed from a weak-kneed wimp to an angry, tough wench. And that was called growth."[6] Such are some of the feelings and the dilemma of the unforgiving. As Smedes observes, "If you cannot free people from their wrongs and see them as the needy people they are, you enslave yourself to your own painful past, and by fastening yourself to the past, you let your hate become your future. You can reverse your future only by releasing other people from their pasts."[7]

Body and emotions will suffer, but what about your spiritual life? What about your relationship to the Lord who loves you? Few warnings in Scripture are worded more strongly than those that confront our refusal or reluctance to forgive.

> For if you forgive men when they sin against you, your heavenly Father will also forgive you. But if you do not forgive men their sins, your Father will not forgive your sins.
>
> Matthew 6:14–15

> "You wicked servant," he said, "I canceled all that debt of yours because you begged me to. Shouldn't you have had mercy on your fellow servant just as I had on you?"
>
> Matthew 18:32–33

But more powerful, if possible, than these warnings should be the appeal to our hearts to remember how deeply we have been forgiven and how costly was the love that accomplished that forgiveness.

> As God's chosen people, holy and dearly loved, clothe yourselves with compassion, kindness, humility, gentleness and patience. Bear with each other and forgive whatever grievances you may have against one another. Forgive as the Lord forgave you.
>
> Colossians 3:12–13

Forgiveness is necessary for freedom from the exhausting attempt to construct and maintain a "balance of payments" kind of relationship between culprit and victim. This contractual arrangement for exchange of social courtesies, this peace conference treaty for cessation of hostilities may make coexistence possible, but it demands constant monitoring for fairness and creates ongoing anxiety about shifts in the balance of power. Forgiveness cuts through the complicated system of checks and balances by bringing in a miraculously refreshing and releasing kind of imbalance. Like God's forgiveness in Christ there is an initiative of grace that liberates, amazes, and wins with the immeasurable power of love.

Before God, the very meaning of our lives depends upon a power from beyond us that sustains, renews, and preserves. Forgiveness is a way of seeing that power in its most radically supportive role . . . to return to the human scene with a resolve not to absolutize any form of calculation as the ultimate path to wholeness. Rights are important, but they are not enough. No strict accounting will do . . . going beyond fairness is the answer. The forgiving initiative may be ours or another's, but the willingness to "hang a little loose" in relationships is precisely what forgiveness requires and what forgiveness brings into the picture. It builds community and relationship by letting things be unequal.[8]

Forgiveness is necessary also for honesty in human relationships. Without that honesty the future of a relationship is always in jeopardy. Honesty comes with confession and appeal for forgiveness on the part of the perpetrator, and honesty comes when the forgiver takes the strides in reinterpreting hurt that introduces new truth into the situation. Up until then our damaged emotions tend to distort how we perceive both the one who hurt us and ourselves. In our woundedness, our perceptions are shaped by our feelings. For healing to occur, our perceptions must be brought into line with reality, with truth. The essence of this reinterpretation of my hurt is seeing those who hurt me as separate from what they did to me and seeing myself as more than my wound.

The power of forgiveness is included in the power of the "truth that will set you free" (John 8:32). Forgiveness is necessary for freedom from the irreversible past. Sometimes our pain comes from the memory of hurt at the hands of those beyond our reach: the person who betrayed us and will never acknowledge it; the "monster" whose ruthless actions destroyed many lives and left countless others scarred; the abusive parent or sibling who died unrepentant and unforgiven. Such persons retain power over our lives if we allow the haunting memories to control us. They have no opportunity to repay us good for the evil they did, even if they could now admit and regret their actions, and our memories cannot be erased. Is there enough miracle in the hard work of forgiveness to bring some peace to our hearts when there can be no redress of our grievances, no access to a hard heart barred against us forever?

The Bible gives us hope for such, telling us that bitter roots do not need to "grow up to cause trouble" (Heb. 12:15) and that at the "throne of grace" there is one who understands hurt and has grace for help in any need (Heb. 4:14–15), which must include even the grace of forgiving. Moreover, there is for us in the gospel such a promise of inclusion in family that our continuing pain from irreversible rejection can begin to fade as we learn more of that familial embrace by our Father and his other children. The Spirit *will* "testify with our spirit that we are God's children . . . heirs of God and co-heirs with Christ . . ." (Rom. 8:16–17). Such rich love makes it possible to live with the unfairness of unsettled emotional accounts.

The crucial necessities of forgiveness are seen in that most intriguing of stories, the parable of the prodigal son. A particularly helpful perspective on forgiveness is found if we enter the story through the mind of the older brother.

There was once a man who had two sons. The younger one said to his father, "Father, give me my share of the estate." So he divided his property between them. Not long after that, the younger son got together all he had, set off for a distant country and there squandered his wealth in wild living. After he had spent everything, there was a severe famine in that whole country, and he began to be in need. So he went and hired himself out to a citizen of that country, who sent him to his field to feed pigs. He longed to fill his stomach with the pods that the pigs were eating, but no one gave him anything. When he came to his senses, he said, "How many of my father's hired men have food to spare, and here I am starving to death! I will set out and go back to my father and say to him: Father, I have sinned, against heaven and against you. I am no longer worthy to be called your son; make me like one of your hired men." So he got up and went to his father. But while he was still a long way off, his father saw him and was filled with compassion for him; he ran to his son, threw his arms around him and kissed him. The son said to him, "Father, I have sinned against heaven and against you. I am no longer worthy to be called your son." But the father said to his servants, "Quick! Bring the best robe and put it on him. Put a ring on his finger and sandals on his feet. Bring the fattened calf and kill it. Let's have a feast and celebrate. For this son of mine was dead and is alive again; he was lost and is found." So they began to celebrate. Meanwhile, the older son was in the field. When he came near the house, he heard music and dancing. So he called one of the servants and asked him what was going on. "Your brother has come," he replied, "and your father has killed the fattened calf because he has him back safe and sound." The older brother became angry and refused to go in. So his father went out and pleaded with him. But he answered his father, "Look! All these years I've been slaving for you and never disobeyed your orders. Yet you never gave me even a young goat so I could celebrate with my friends. But when this son of yours who has squandered your property with prostitutes comes home, you kill the fattened calf for him!" "My son," the father said, "you are always with me, and everything I have is yours. But we had to celebrate and be glad, because this brother of yours was dead and is alive again; he was lost and is found."

Luke 15:11–32

We can use the older brother to clobber ourselves with guilt: If we cannot forgive someone we are just like this proud, angry, holier-than-thou, wretched brother standing outside in the dark, hurting the heart of his loving father! Or we can heap scorn on the older brother, perhaps because we know Jesus is telling the story to the Pharisees and we choose to identify the older brother—not ourselves—with them.

But let us not miss the tone of the parable. Jesus is much more gentle toward this character in his story than we usually are. He uses the older brother to speak a lovingly urgent appeal to the Pharisees to join his celebration of the salvation of the lost. The older brother is not a bad guy, he is the hardworking son of his father who has been hurt, has seen his father hurt, and needs, like each of us, to learn how to forgive and be reconciled to those who have hurt us.

The parable is an incomplete story. Jesus may have wanted to creatively stimulate our imagination and have us write the ending in our own minds. Suppose the older brother were to be reconciled to his younger brother. What hard work would be necessary to be part of the miracle of forgiveness?

First, he would have to recognize a foundation for their relationship. If he would listen to his father's poignant appeal he would be reminded of that foundation: "My son . . . this brother of yours. . . ." (vv. 31–32). The father echoes and calls back for reconsideration his older son's bitter allusion to "this son of yours who has squandered your property" (v. 30). The father is trying to say, "You are *both* my children!" There is the foundation for a reconciliation; they both need the love and forgiveness of the same father.

Second, to be reconciled to his brother, the older of the sons would need to ask the father's help to see his brother with new eyes. If he was not yet able to trust his brother or the motives that brought him home, at least he would need to see his brother in the present not just through eyes of the past: "This brother of yours was dead and is alive again; he was lost and is found" (v. 32). The older brother is saying to his father: "How dare he come back! Don't you see the injustice?" The father is saying to his son: "He's back! He's back! Don't you see the miracle?" *Again, to move toward reconciliation the older brother would have to accept and begin small steps in forgiveness.* "The older brother became angry and refused to go in. So his father went out and pleaded with him" (v. 28).

The father must dearly have wanted his sons reconciled completely, but all that seems to be the issue at the moment, that is until the older brother widened the issue, was would he join the party? He could be angry still, but would he just let the distance between him and his brother decrease for a while? Would he try a first step?

In the pilgrimage of forgiveness we need to start where we are, not where we would be if we had some imagined greater strength of will, but where we are now.

Writing of the process of his reconciliation with a friend after a painful and confusing estrangement, Dr. Lewis Smedes remembers: "Forgiveness did come. It came by fits and starts, trickles, driblets of it seeping down the drains of our mutual resentments, but it did come . . . with an unexpected meeting here, a gesture there, the exchange of a greeting, and a hint that better feelings were beginning to flow. We floundered into forgiving . . . Not a triumph of forgiver's art, I agree. But healing often comes on the wings of trivia . . . Ordinary people forgive best if they go at it in bits and pieces, and for specific acts . . . forgiving anything at all is a minor miracle; forgiving carte blanche is silly. Nobody can do it. Except God."[9]

Jesus may want us to ask ourselves this about the story of the Prodigal: what might have happened if the older brother had at least gone with his father into the house, for even a few minutes?

Third, to be reconciled to his brother the older son would have to accept the scars caused by his brother's selfish desertion of the family. By this we mean, first of all, that he must absorb the loss caused by his brother's action. The brother is justly and appropriately angry. His younger brother had betrayed their father's kindness and left him to pick up the pieces: "All these years I've been slaving. . . ." (v. 29). The father, in turn, acknowledges the unfairness of the situation, saying: "My son, you are always with me. . . ." (v. 31), thus assuring his son, "I know, you too have been wronged, we're not ignoring that. I know this is hard for you."

There is no argument that the son's anger is excessive. The argument is, though, that his anger can now begin to give way to something more satisfying, a new future of peace, if he will learn to leave "loose ends dangling," "the scales off balance," "to accept a score that neither of them can make come out even." Accepting the scars also means learning to trust his father with what it costs to forgive. He will need to hear the power and promise in his father's words: "Everything I have is yours" (v. 31). He must not fear the future; he won't really lose by forgiving, though it may seem so now. The father is saying, as our Father says to us, "Trust the same generosity in me for you that you see me give to your brother."

Related to this is the fact that the guarantee for the future comes only from the father. There is no information in the parable to tell us what the returning brother may be able to give of himself to his older sibling. He has come home to the *father*; that's all we know (v. 18). The younger may be capable of doing very little to improve his relationship to the older.

But the older brother still needs to trust his father, absorb his losses, and forgive his brother because he needs to forgive for his father's sake—and for his own sake. We already know the dangers to the health of body and soul that come from the refusal to forgive, but there is another reason woven into this marvelous parable, a reason why forgiveness is for our own sake: We ought not to miss the celebration!

As originally told by Jesus, the context of this story was the muttering of his disciples that Jesus welcomed sinners. Seeing their grim mood, he told this and two other stories, each revolving around a gathering for joyful celebration (Luke 15:5–9, 23). When we forgive someone who hurt us, we join the rejoicing heart of God, we share his contagious pleasure in showing mercy, we reflect the love that gave us our own pardon and received us back from our own rebellion. It is no accident that Jesus told these stories featuring the joy of restoration. He wants us where he is, at the welcome home feast!

The Feelings of the Unforgiven

Unforgiven guilt manifests itself in a gamut of unpleasant feelings. These fall into three general groupings: fear of punishment or a self-inflicted punishment; loss of self-esteem; loneliness, rejection, or isolation. S. Bruce Narramore summarizes some of the answers given when people are asked how they felt when they felt guilty. Here are some of their replies:

> Scared, uneasy. Tense, like maybe I'm going to get caught. A feeling of impending punishment. Like if somebody finds out I'll be punished and they will scream what I've done to everyone. My mind has a tendency to kick itself several times. Disgusted with myself. Like a raunchy person or a complete failure. Stupid, low, remorseful. Miserable and ashamed. Rotten inside, worthless. A feeling of separation. Lonely and very frustrated. I feel nobody loves me— especially God. I find it hard to like myself. Depressed and separated from others.[10]

It seems that many of the same feelings experienced by the victim of wrongs are also the experience of the remorseful perpetrator who has not yet come to accept forgiveness: loneliness, anxiety, depression, eating disorders, sexual dysfunction, anger, self-hatred; these and more are the feelings of the unforgiven. The Scripture would see these feelings in a Christian as being part of "the spirit of bondage" dominating the one who does not understand the power of grace or believe that forgiving grace is available in their case.

For you did not receive a spirit that makes you a slave again to fear, but you received the Spirit who makes you sons. And by him we cry, "Abba, Father." The Spirit himself testifies with our spirit that we are God's children. Now if we are children, then we are heirs—heirs of God and coheirs with Christ. . . .

                                                                    Romans 8:15–17a

Forgiveness is the answer to feelings of guilt and anger. A refusal to forgive is to nourish these ravenously destructive feelings. Forgiveness is not easy. It is, however, both possible and necessary if we are to be whole.

A Pastoral Priority

With the promise of such freedom for the Christian, it is obvious that pastors must make the understanding of forgiveness central to their care for the members of the body of Christ. It is so crucial because spiritual growth in believers may be stunted when those persons are unforgiven or unforgiving. The unforgiven strains to hear the Spirit's call to peace and wholeness. The unforgiving cannot grow into the image of Christ when the most Christlike virtue is resisted. Neither can hear the preached Word with open mind and heart, when like the seed in Jesus' parable of the soils it is choked by the thorns of resentment or fear (Mark 4:1–20).

A pastor's concern for the unity of the body should make forgiveness an essential topic of study. Most have known the disappointment of members leaving the fellowship because of unresolved personal conflict with other members. Many have heard the complaint, "I just can't be in the sanctuary and worship when I look across the aisle and see _____there!" The pastor protests, "Why not? Christ is here in our worship, isn't he? You come to worship him!" They reply, "If he is here, I cannot see him because I see _____, and think of the wrong I suffered from that person!"

Suspicion, cynicism, hurt pride, angry memory of pain, and inability to trust, all can damage the body of Christ from within. The admonition for all members of a congregation rests most heavily on the pastor: "See to it that no one misses the grace of God and that no bitter root grows up to cause trouble and defile many" (Heb. 12:15).

Counseling is well defined as "being-with," a basic metaphor of the Christian faith and the essence of the covenant relationship that God offers his people. "And if God offers his people his faithful presence in the midst of their suffering, brokenness, and struggles, so too the counselor can offer to be with those who seek his or her help. Being with others in their existential struggles captures the heart of what counseling is all about.[11] Where in the counseling encounter with human need does the pastor have greater opportunity to be with the counselee in looking at the cross of Christ and the good news of reconcilatory healing than in dealing with the necessity of forgiveness?

Such is the necessity of forgiveness!

4

The Difficulty
of Forgiveness

It would be quite hard to forgive a man who is "surly and mean in his dealings"; a man who is "such a wicked man that no one can talk to him." David found it hard to forgive the man described this way in 1 Samuel 25. This rich man, Nabal, had been treated with kindness by David, whose soldiers had protected Nabal's herdsmen from raiding parties. Nabal, in turn, refused to give aid to David and his hungry men during their exile in the desert and had slandered and insulted them. David determined to have revenge and is making his way to the desired slaughter when he is met by Nabal's wife. Abigail intercedes, pleading for David to forgive (v. 28), to trust God's care and grace ("bound securely in the bundle of the living by the Lord your God," v. 29), to trust his cause to God (v. 30), and to seek the lifelong blessing of a conscience free from vengeful bloodshed (v. 31).

Though David relents, accepts her plea, and abandons his plans for revenge, he has anger left over and he cannot help being glad when ten days later Nabal is dead by the hand of God ("Praise be to the Lord, who has upheld my cause against Nabal for treating me with contempt," v. 39).

71

We New Testament believers may look back at David through the cross of Jesus Christ and wonder why David, as a believer in the same God, could not forgive Nabal more completely, as Jesus forgave his enemies. We look back at David through the window of the writings of the apostles and want him to display more patience, kindness, and love—more fruit of the Spirit. We need to remember David's place in the unfolding of salvation history. In God's patient preparation of his people for the ultimate gospel, David's rugged mercy to Nabal surely qualifies as an act of "far-enough-for-the-light-he-had" forgiveness.

Perhaps the story of David, Nabal, and Abigail is better seen as being about not taking vengeance, not acting upon vindictive feeling. David did that much and more for he, indeed, turned from vengeful rage to committing his cause to the promises of God for his future, based upon his recognition of God's faithfulness in his past. This much is an equivalent in David to the spirit of new covenant forgiveness: Abigail, in effect, said to David, Just as God has been good to you, so you be good to us (v. 28–29); and we are told to forgive "just as in Christ God forgave" (Eph. 4:32).

We may struggle with anger as did David and for us, too, just not yielding to our vindictive desires may be a long, early, and real step in forgiveness. Whatever else we may see in this story, we do see an example of the fact that forgiveness is difficult!

David also illustrates the difficulties on the other side of life's experience with forgiveness: receiving it. His Psalm 32 is framed in rejoicing in God's forgiveness ("Blessed . . . Blessed . . . Rejoice . . . be glad . . . sing," vv. 1–2, 11), but between the first and the final cries of joy we find David's testimony to the feelings he suffered while he delayed confessing his sin and accepting God's grace ("wasted . . . groaning . . . heavy . . . strength was sapped," vv. 3–4). We also find his admonition to us to avoid his painful experience by receiving "the Lord's unfailing love" (vv. 5–10). David gives us a picture of physical and emotional torment and begs us not to be stubborn in the face of mercy. Although David's difficulty remembered in Psalm 32 may have been primarily that of acknowledging his sin, a comparison with Psalm 51 leads us to believe that he also suffered an in-between period when, having confessed, he was however, not yet assured of God's complete forgiveness ("Do not cast me from your presence or take your Holy Spirit from me. Restore to me the joy of your salvation," vv. 11–12). There seems to be a note of uncertainty and tentativeness in these words. It is a plea, a hoped for but not yet realized confidence that God will restore him to his favor.

The very conviction of sin that makes confession and the receiving of forgiveness possible may create fear that one has sinned beyond grace. David seems to know that his sin is so heinous that only God can accomplish effective cleansing of his conscience ("wash me, and I will be whiter than snow," v. 7). The expression is not one used for washing oneself, but one that refers to the washing of clothes by treading them. It suggests not a polite rinse but a thorough scrub, which presupposes that the object of washing is in a thoroughly dishevelled state . . . This is how the psalmist feels.

Only God can forgive, but will he? My fears and shame may deafen me to the answer. Receiving forgiveness may be hard!

Why Is Forgiveness So Difficult to Give?

There are a number of reasons why it is so difficult to forgive another person. Some of these are associated with our anger over the hurt done to us, while others come from our fears of the process of forgiveness, its responsibilities and vulnerabilities.

Anger may be a recurring feeling even after one has decided to forgive. "When you are wronged, that wrong becomes an indestructible reality of your life. When you forgive, you heal your hate for the person who created that reality. But you do not change the facts, and you do not undo all of their consequences. The dead stay dead; the wounded are often crippled still. The reality of evil and its damage to human beings is not magically undone and it can still make us very mad . . . A man does not forget that his father abused him as a child. A woman does not forget that her boss lied to her about her future in the company. You do not forget that a person you loved has taken cheap advantage of you and dropped you when the relationship was not paying off . . . And when you do remember what happened, how can you remember except in anger?"[1]

In our understandable anger we may resist extending forgiveness because of the ambiguities and inequities involved.

It seems unfair that forgiveness is a willing relinquishment of certain rights, often hard fought for rights. In forgiveness you choose not to demand your rights of complete redress for the hurt you have suffered.

"Forgiveness is not a neatly balanced relationship. It exalts the one who forgives to such an important place that dependence on that person shapes life differently. It builds community by letting things be unequal and open-ended. . . . This asymmetrical, unequal pattern in forgiveness makes forgiveness troubling, . . . a kind of cheap way out; certainly it is always tempting to make it work the old-fashioned way where everyone earns what they get."[2] Forgiveness seems to place too much of the burden of reconciliation upon the one who suffered the injustice and damage rather than upon the perpetrator.

In my justified anger I may feel that there are wrongs which prevent complete reconciliation. How far must I go? Writing in *The Christian Century*, Richard P. Lord tells of a woman who came to him with questions about how she could forgive a man who murdered her four sons. A few years earlier, a group of young men had gotten high on drugs, broken into her farmhouse home, killed her boys, and shot and left her for dead. Now one of the convicted criminals had written to tell her that he had become a Christian and asked for her forgiveness.

Her questions had to do with whether forgiving this man meant she must have any dealings with him. Lord reports that she was "not open to a future with those who killed her children. She had no relationship with them before the murders and she desires none now. She hopes they create for themselves a positive future, but one that does not include her. Betty Jane is quite ready to affirm that God is merciful and is hopeful that the murderers of her sons will find a genuine relationship with God. But don't ask her to be responsible for their salvation. Don't ask her to go to them and judge their hearts. Let a representative of the church assume that burden."[3] If forgiving meant including them in her life, she felt forgiving would be impossible.

At the opposite end of the spectrum, it may be that the most difficult person to forgive will be one we have loved and trusted much before they hurt and betrayed us. Love does not, in fact, necessarily make forgiveness easy. Love can complicate the process of forgiveness. Leon Morris observes:

> Let us suppose that some passing tramp breaks into your home and steals something you value highly. In due course he is arrested. He denies that he robbed you, but his guilt is clear. He is caught with the goods, let us say. There is no doubt whatever. You would say to yourself, "Perhaps this poor fellow has never had much of a chance in life. I am a Christian. I have been forgiven much and I ought to forgive." So you forgive him. It is as easy as that.
>
> But suppose that the person who robbed you and lied to you was not a passing tramp, whom you have never seen before and will never see again, but your best friend. Now the way of forgiveness is harder. And the thing that makes it harder, the thing that complicates the situation is just the fact of your love. Your whole being cries out for the restoration of the earlier state of fellowship. With all your heart you want to forgive. But precisely because you love your friend so much, the way to the forgiveness you are so ready to offer is not easy. And if instead of your friend, the one who robbed you and lied to you was your son, one to whom you owe the duty of showing the best way in life, as well as one whom you love with all your heart, then the way of forgiveness may well be very complicated indeed. Love will make forgiveness certain, but it will not make it easy.[4]

Again my anger may flow to a large extent not from personal resentment or sorrow, but from a true sense of the rightness of punishment for those who ruthlessly injure others. I may be genuinely concerned for the preservation of moral responsibility in family, business, church, community, and nation. I may regard punishment as a necessary deterrent to the culprit repeating his crime with other victims. Should my forgiveness release the doer of harm upon someone else?

Finally, the negative feelings that accompany my anger can be invigorating, can make me feel alive. I may not be ready to give up the sense of power I feel over the person who hurt me, who may have controlled my life in their abuse of selfishness. I felt weak and vulnerable; now my anger has restored a sense of control over my own life and I fear forgiveness will mean giving up too much of my new power. Also, there is a fresh feeling of moral superiority in my relationship with the person who hurt me, I am shamed no longer, and I have gained moral high ground that I do not wish to surrender.[5]

Resolving Difficulties with Forgiveness

How do we resolve these difficulties? To begin with, and as already indicated, do not be surprised by fresh waves of anger. The goal with our anger is to move beyond malice, to abandon opportunities for vindictive striking back. Though you cannot erase the past, you can get beyond being obsessed with it, being driven by it. In the process of forgiveness you will become less and less focused upon the remembered pain. Your anger will, in time, have less enduring emotional energy. As God gives you hope for a future free for new beginnings, you will find yourself gladly less responsive to the memories of old pain.

When you struggle with the inequities of forgiveness, with the heavier burden that rests upon you, the forgiver, remember that this hard work is also a miracle. God has grace for such sacrifices. It is he who made suffering for the sake of another person a powerful part of forgiveness when he took the punishment for our sins upon himself. It is, therefore, possible that we who "live by the Spirit" should be able to "keep in step with the Spirit" (Gal. 5:22–26) as he enables our new choices in life.

The imbalance in relationships, accepted as part of our forgiving journey, will not be a manipulative, obligation-creating way of controlling another person, though we must avoid that temptation. "In contrast, real forgiveness accepts vicarious suffering as an unavoidable by-product of concern and respect for the other person. It is not suffering sought for its own sake or as a means of asserting power. It is suffering that is taken on as the price of a hopeful future . . . Forgiveness enriches the future with genuinely new possibilities . . . potential for change, for growth, for renewal."[6]

This is grace-enabled gift giving when there may be little reason to feel love or to expect that love will be adequately returned. Walter Wangerin Jr. emphasizes the crucial power in this giving of undeserved kindness as he deals with forgiving in marriage: "Only when the spouse has heard his sin, so that he might anticipate, under the law, some retribution, but receives instead the gestures of love—only then can he begin to change and grow in the same humility which his wife has shown him."[7]

When there have been wrongs that seem to have destroyed all possibility for reconciliation, we may have to find our answers in David's experience with Nabal. We may have to do what we can to move on to a future without vengeance and trust that God, who will be there in our future will help us to a conscience finally free from hatred. We may have to pray for grace to pray for grace! God can bring us to the place, like the mother of the murdered boys, where we can hope the culprits will seek and receive his forgiveness even though we are not yet up to being the channel of blessing to them ourselves. Perhaps the apostle Paul had such realism in mind when, while commanding that we "not repay anyone evil for evil," added, *"If it is possible, as far as depends on you,* live at peace with everyone" (Rom. 12:17–18).

When the hurt seems overwhelming because it has come from someone you love, perhaps the key to forgiving is to pray and strive for perspective. Must the offense, betrayal that it is, destroy *all* previous bonds of love between you? Complicated though forgiving such a person may be, try to be specific in your memory of their offenses. And add to such a list another roster, the reasons you have loved them in the past. The Holy Spirit, through Paul, suggests the power of such list-making: "Whatever is true, whatever is noble, whatever is admirable—if anything is excellent or praiseworthy—think about such things . . . And the God of peace will be with you" (Phil. 4:8–9). And also remember the spiritual power of covenant-keeping when we turn for help to our God, who has kept his covenant of grace with his people through all their rebellions. Hear him cry to Israel, "When Israel was a child, I loved him . . . How can I give you up, Ephraim?" (Hos. 11:1, 8). Because God has such a heart he can teach us how not to give up those who break our hearts.

A helpful approach in this is reviewed in Rinda G. Rogers' discussion of "Forgiveness and the Healing of Family." Rogers refers extensively to work by Margaret Cortrones who suggests that forgiveness is an act of relationship and is a multifaceted act or process. She outlines that process in three parts.

First, "turning," that is a turning toward oneself to acknowledge not only one's own role in the family's damaged relationships, but also one's own sense of being damaged or even abandoned by the family.

Second, "facing," that is, facing reciprocal indebtedness. This refers to hearing the other's story, either through the imagination if the person is not available or through actual listening if contact can be made.

Third, "reclaiming," which is identifying and owning past and present resources in the relationship. It involves the acceptance of one's legacy by acknowledging what one has given and received in the history of the family, the recall of what existed between the participants in the past, including the invisible loyalties that bound the family together for better or worse.[8]

Are there elements in the relationship that have worked for both parties in the past? Can those elements be part of the rebuilding, no matter how slowly and carefully, of the relationship? Perhaps these steps may help in the regaining of perspective and the reawakening of memories of love, shared in the form of bonds, that the offense need not also destroy though it has broken much.

When we feel that punishment must not be neglected, we must remember that we ought not assume that we are the ones to do the punishing by withholding forgiveness. That would bring us perilously close to crossing the line between punishment and revenge. Retribution is God's business, not ours (Rom. 12:17–19). Dan Hamilton writes:

> Vengeance in the Bible is described in detail, hoped for, prayed for, promised. And it is left securely and solely in God's hands. He has reserved it for himself. There are reasons for this. James tells us that "the anger of man does not work the righteousness of God" (1:20). When I was young, I helped my father build things in his workshop. I could do some of the work and use some of the tools, but I was reminded, "Keep your hands off the power tools. They are good tools, and useful in my hands to do what I want done, but they are too powerful and dangerous for you to use." Revenge is a spiritual power tool fitted to God's hand alone.[9]

Related to this may be my resistance to abandoning my anger which gives me the feeling of at last being in control. For long I may have felt victimized and helpless; now it feels good and right to find the "tables turned." The answer to this may lie in understanding that what I really need control over is the power of the past to cruelly influence my life. The hurtful memories, not necessarily the repentant perpetrator, is what I now have in my power.

To forgive is not necessarily to extend unconditional trust. Genuine forgiveness means that I no longer hold the hurt over the head of the other person. It does not mean that I must assume that I will never again be hurt by them, nor does it mean that I should never take steps to minimize this possibility.

Additionally, I must realize that the perceived value from the empowerment anger seems to give me must be put in perspective with the possible ultimate cost to my own spirit, and possibly my innocent friends or family, of malice unrelinquished: "See to it that no one misses the grace of God and that no bitter root grows up to cause trouble and defile many" (Heb. 12:15).

There are also difficulties in forgiveness that come from our fears of the process. Some of these fears are closely related to the handling of our anger, so we may have already dealt in part with the resolving of them; for instance, the problem of vulnerability to becoming a victim again or the fear that forgiveness means we now have to "feel good about" a person who has done monstrous wrong.

Beyond these there may also be fear of not being able to stick it out. Forgiveness takes time, may consist of repeated acts of fresh beginnings after new disappointments, and we grow tired of difficult relationships. Already exhausted emotionally by the shock of the wrong done you, there may seem to be no energy left for the long haul of forgiving. There's nothing left in me to give you any more, may be your honest feeling.

Add to this the memory of previous failure in an experiment with forgiving. You tried to forgive a little, back before the record of wrongs mounted up, and you found it very unsatisfying. Nothing seemed better. What will protect you from such discouragement now?

Again, add the fact that the process of forgiveness may require many times of confrontation between culprit and victim. Such confrontation is tricky. Sincerity is hard to measure and you run the risk of being manipulated. On your part, bringing with you even unconscious bitterness will cause your words to quickly become "boiling oil and not the oil of mercy. A cornered creature is remarkably perceptive . . . will sense the hidden attack . . . grow defensive . . . fight the hurt you bring . . . division between you will increase . . ."[10]

What is the use? Would not distance between you, probably permanent distance, be the least hurtful solution?

The answer to these fears must be realistic. Perhaps to admit that what you fear is true may be the best approach. Forgiveness may be a long, long road to travel; there may not be any protection from repeated discouragement and many confrontations may mean trial, error, and frequent failure.

But now comes the grace of God. A large component of that which is created in your spirit by the grace of God is hope. There may be continuing pain, but it can be hopeful pain! Pain that feels like it is part of a birthing labor, and for the hope set before you, you endure that labor pain. God is called "the God of hope" who is able to make us "overflow with hope by the power of the Holy Spirit" (Rom. 15:13).

Key, too, will be your own experience of forgiveness. God's forgiveness of your sins is not only a model for you to copy ("as in Christ God forgave you," Eph. 4:32), but his forgiveness is a source of your power to forgive. Christ crucified and risen is a deep well of water within your life, water for the person thirsty for your forgiveness ("the water I give will become in him a spring of water . . . streams of living water will flow from within him," John 4:14; 7:38).

If you find it hard to forgive, it will help if you think about the other side of the struggle: how hard it may be to receive your forgiveness! And how hard it may be to receive—to truly believe the possibility of God's forgiveness.

The other set of difficulties in forgiveness is in receiving it. The hard-work miracle may be hard to believe as a miracle. Who qualifies for a miracle? Certainly, we think, not a guilty perpetrator of pain in the lives of those whose trust we have betrayed. How can God forgive what *I* have done? Why do I find it so hard to believe that God's mercy can outlast my sinful ugliness?

The answers and solutions may lie in following three steps:

1. Realize the hidden motives you may have in fearing to rest in God's sheer mercy.
2. Remember the tactics of the enemy of your soul's peace and learn how to overcome them.
3. Reexamine the reality and integrity of the forgiveness provided for you in Jesus Christ.

I must also realize that among the factors in my resistance to forgiveness may be a failure to forgive myself. I may be using a refusal to believe God's forgiveness as a mask for self-punishment. We learn from our parents that wrongdoing deserves punishment, and that became a principle adopted for a lifetime. The need for payment by punishment also grows out of depression and anger with ourselves for having failed to live up to our own expectations. Another habit of the heart is to attempt appeasement: If I punish myself, maybe God will not. Self-punishing sacrifice may be offered in the form of self-denial, self-neglect, or self-hatred.

So deeply ingrained in our thinking is the idea that everything must be paid for. There is "no free lunch." Even forgiveness, apparently free and given in love, must have a catch to it somewhere. The ultimate hidden cost may be more than we are willing or able to pay.

The problem with all this is that my ability to punish myself adequately may run out. With each self-accusing encounter with guilt, payment is made from "a diminishing reserve of dignity and sense of personal worth." Self-dislike and anger against self mounts. Self-punishment is a poor, false, and potentially disastrous substitute for the grace of God!

I also need to realize that a refusal to accept forgiveness can be a form of idolatry and pride. Boldly put, Am I such a unique exception in the world that I can handle my redemption better than God? I would rather do so perhaps because the alternative is to accept that I am not the nice person I had thought! I need to hear David's plea in Psalm 32:9, "Do not be like the horse or the mule. . . ."

A further step in accepting forgiveness is to remember that Satan is a lying accuser. If my problem is not refusal to acknowledge my sin or a compulsion to be my own judge and jailer, then it may be that I am prey to the accusations of the Evil One as he seeks to keep me from assurance of God's grace.

Scripture calls Satan our "enemy" (adversary), "accuser," and "slanderer" (cf. 1 Tim. 5:14; 1 Peter 5:8; Rev. 12:10). But perhaps he does not accuse us to ourselves as often as he accuses God to us. He seeks to impugn the character of God, so as to discourage us or cause us to doubt. To do this he misrepresents God and God's Word, casting doubt upon God's love, grace, intentions, presence, and forgiveness. The Devil always points us away from Christ in his accusations, either to get us to excuse self or dwell upon self. On the other hand, the Holy Spirit points us to Christ, and if he convicts of sin, he also seeks to convince us of grace.

Satan twists Scripture. For example, passages on God's wrath, warning against careless sinners or wicked opponents of the Gospel, will be used by Satan to depress or intimidate struggling, fearful Christians. Satan confuses doctrine. For example, he will seek to get us to confuse troubling sin with reigning sin; sin as rebellion in the Christian life with sin reigning in the unbeliever's life. (Rom. 6:11–14, "Sin shall not be your master.") How do you meet his accusations?

1. Address the power of sin instead of the shame of sin. Study what it is doing to you more than how it makes you feel. Master the topic in Romans, chapters 5 through 8.
2. Work to keep your conscience clean through confession (Acts 24:16; 1 Tim. 1:19; Heb. 9:14).
3. Fix your eyes upon the evidences of grace in your life, past and present. Search the Scriptures for and meditate upon the promises of grace. "In your temptations run to the promises: they are your Lord's branches hanging over the water, that our Lord's silly, half-drowned children may take a grip of them. . . ." (Samuel Rutherford, writing from exile where he often fought doubts and discouragement).
4. Share your struggle over guilt with another believer and ask them to pray for your assurance of forgiveness.
5. Above all, realize that Satan cannot accuse you, a Christian, before God! God may convict you of sin in order to bring you to confession and cleansing, but he will not listen to the accusations of Satan and change his mind about your salvation! "Who will bring any charge against those who God has cho-

sen? It is God who justifies. Who is he that condemns? Christ Jesus, who died—more than that, who was raised to life—is at the right hand of God and is also interceding for us" (Rom. 8:33–34).

This brings us to the third step in being able to receive forgiveness: Reexamine the forgiveness provided for you in Jesus Christ to discover again that it is not fragile and conditional.

As in Romans 8, quoted above, in 1 John 2:1 we find a powerful statement about the confidence we may have in God's forgiving of us. "My dear children, I write this to you so that you will not sin. But if anybody does sin, we have one who speaks to the Father in our defense—Jesus Christ the Righteous One."

Who speaks in your defense? "Jesus Christ, the Righteous One." To whom does he speak in your defense? "The Father." Does the Father need to be begged in your behalf? No, forgiving is the Father's idea from the beginning. There is a holy collusion! "This is love: not that we loved God, but that he loved us and sent his Son as an atoning sacrifice for our sins" (1 John 4:10).

Jesus' *presence* is a continual "speaking." Not as though he has to constantly be there to restrain God, like a kindly older brother who can calm down the temper of an angry parent. No. He is there as God's greatest joy, the Redeemer of the children the Father loves. Justice has been done, evil's doom is sealed, the runaway child has been rescued, and love can celebrate. Jesus, righteous himself, and the answer to the guilt of those who trust him, stands before the throne fully accepted by God. There is courtroom language in this verse, but we must be careful not to impart with our imagination the experiences we may have had in observing human courts. There is no hustle of a busy courtroom and a frazzled judge trying to keep current with an overwhelming caseload. Rather, in your behalf is the great calm of heaven and the continual evidence that sets you free, the presence of the eternal Sacrifice!

We, who seek to counsel with the gospel as our greatest resource, must be those who know our own sinfulness, who can make a realistic and humble response to our own guilt without giving in to the temptations of repression, denial, or despair. We must be deeply convinced that healing is found in the magnificent grace of our forgiving God who comes to us, seeks us out, and pursues us even as we flee from him, and brings the healing which we so desperately need and can find lastingly in no other source. In his extremely valuable work on personal holiness, J. I. Packer points out the essential role of forgiveness:

> We have seen, finally, that personal holiness is personal wholeness—the ongoing reintegration of our disintegration and disordered personhood as we pursue our goal of single-minded Jesus-likeness; the increasing mastery of our life that comes as we learn to give it back to God and away to others; the deepening joy of finding worthwhileness in even the most tedious and mundane tasks when tackled for the glory of God and the good of other people; and the peace that pours from the discovery that, galling as failure in itself is, we can handle our failures—we can afford to fail, as some daringly put it—because all along *we live precisely by being forgiven, and we are not required at any stage to live any other way.*[11]

Part 2

Facilitating Forgiveness

The Role of Forgiveness in Pastoral Care

The importance of forgiveness in Strategic Pastoral Counseling is based on two facts—its centrality to the gospel and its essential role in the healing of emotional wounds. The former point was made in the first chapter. The second point, the foundational role of forgiveness in the resolution of the sorts of problems typically brought to pastors, will be the focus of the present chapter.

Coping with Life's Disappointments

It is a rare person who reaches adulthood without realizing the inevitability of hurts and disappointments in life. The Old Testament patriarch Job made the point with disarming realism when he stated that "Man is born for trouble as surely as sparks fly upward" (Job 5:7). This prognostication is echoed by a more recent realist, Murphy, whose law reminds us that if something can go wrong, it will.

Pastoral counselors know this law well. Along with other counselors, their calling is to listen to people talk about the things that have gone wrong in their lives. Loss of jobs, illness, marital tensions, problems with children, disappointment in relationships, financial reversals, and the death of a loved one are but a few of the "things gone wrong" that are routinely presented to pastors.

The common component in this diverse list of things that can and do go wrong is that life has not turned out as hoped. Not always is it immediately obvious to the person that they had, in fact, been operating with expectations which are now disappointed. However, their reactions betray an underlying expectation. On reflection, this expectation may be seen to be totally unrealistic (such as, "I expect to live in good health forever," or, "I expect my son to be like me") or it may be more reasonable (such as, "I expect my friends to always treat me with respect," or, "I expect my husband to remain faithful to me"). But either consciously or subconsciously people do have expectations about their lives, and their reactions to life's disappointments can in one sense be understood as reactions to these expectations.

The manner in which a person reacts to an experience of life which has not turned out as hoped for depends on a great variety of factors. One of these is the nature of the expectation. Expectations vary on a continuum from demand to hope. At the demand end of this continuum, the expected experience is viewed as an inalienable right. At the hope end, the expected experience is viewed as more of a wished for outcome. People tend to respond to expectations of the "demand" variety primarily with anger. In contrast, they more typically respond to expectations of the "hope" variety with sadness. Since most expectations contain elements of both of these forms of anticipation, it is most common for people to respond to disappointments with a mixture of both anger and sadness.

Much of pastoral counseling is helping people deal redemptively with such experiences of disappointment. Whether these disappointments take the form of disappointment with others or with self, the central dynamic in the redemptive and healing process will always be forgiveness.

Disappointment with Others

The major cause of emotional wounds is disappointment with others. Whether it be an unfaithful husband or one who seems to love his work more than his family, a wife who has lost her faith and become cynical of anything to do with religion, a business partner whose behaviors seem to violate the basic values and agreements of the partnership, a close friend who appears to have forgotten the friendship, or a child who is alienated from the family, the feeling of disappointment with others is in each case the core of the experienced hurt.

But as noted above, the emotional response to disappointment is sufficiently variable that it is not always apparent that the underlying experience is one of disappointment. Sadness, the core affect in most people's response to disappointment, may be masked by anger, and it, in turn, may be masked by chronic suspiciousness, jealousy, self-pity, impatience, cynicism, or depression. Usually at the root of these feelings and behaviors, one can find a sense of having been disappointed in a relationship and it is this core experience which usually must be resolved in order for the person to experience healing of the emotional wounds.

Recognizing the essential nature of the counselee's problem is an act of discernment. Such discernment, crucial in any counseling but made even more essential by the short-term, focused nature of Strategic Pastoral Counseling, is both a gift of the Holy Spirit and a skill to be developed. To fail to identify the underlying feelings of disappointment will usually result in a failure to resolve the more superficial feelings which are protecting the counselee from the core disappointment. While anger, depression, and other masks of this core of inner hurt are often painful, the discomfort associated with them is almost always easier to face than the pain associated with the disappointment.

The reason for this is that disappointment in another person is usually experienced as a violation of a trust. An unfaithful spouse or an unjust employer are both perceived as violating an implicit contract, a contract which specified, among other things, fairness and fidelity. People feel hurt when they perceive that others are not playing by the rules of these implicit contracts because they trust that others will treat them fairly. As C. S. Lewis notes, even the most thorough-going ethical relativist who disavows any external reference point for morality, quickly discovers the operation of internal standards of morality the moment these are violated by the behavior of another.

Resolution of the feelings which tend to mask emotional injury is extremely difficult without identifying the underlying sense of disappointment because without such an identification, forgiveness seems irrelevant. What sense does it make to speak of forgiveness in relation to depression, self-pity, chronic suspiciousness, or jealousy? Without recognizing that, at core, the person is angry at someone whom they perceive has trampled over their rights and violated a trust (either implicit or explicit), they are left stuck with that anger. Forgiveness of another person becomes relevant only when they recognize that there is another person who needs their forgiveness. This is the first step in Strategic Pastoral Counseling with problems of interpersonal disappointment.

To illustrate the way in which a Strategic Pastoral Counselor should seek to deal with masked disappointments, consider a thirty-five-year-old man whom we will call Paul. Paul contacted his pastor by phone and asked to meet in order to discuss some concerns he was facing. Knowing that he had just been asked to serve as an elder in the congregation, his pastor assumed that this might be part of what he wished to discuss. This guess turned out to be correct. When they got together the next day, Paul indicated that he was reluctant to accept this position, stating as his reason the fact that he wasn't feeling very good about where he was spiritually. Exploration of what this meant revealed that Paul was feeling little interest in prayer, bible reading, or even church attendance. However, he also indicated that this was part of a pattern; in reality, he was finding nothing in his life to be of much interest at present.

The pastor showed wisdom in deciding to pursue this last revelation, declining the temptation to approach the matter, at least at this point, as simply one of spiritual lethargy. Asking if Paul could tell him more about what he was feeling, it became clear that he was somewhat depressed. Paul reported that he was feeling discouraged and not liking himself very much and that his work in particular had become very unsatisfying for him. Following up this reference to work by asking what had changed in that area finally led to the fact that he had been passed over for a promotion and that this had been the turning point in his feelings about work and himself.

At last they had reached the core problem. Simply focusing on the feelings of spiritual disinterest would not have allowed Paul to confront the deeper feelings of disappointment, hurt, and anger, which were associated with the experience of having not been promoted. Paul had not purposefully hidden this deeper issue from the pastor. First and foremost, he had been hiding it from himself. He had been, and remained for some time, very reluctant to admit that he was depressed. He had been running his life in accordance with a script that dictated that Christians must not be depressed and he had great trouble acknowledging his real reactions to the failure to receive the promotion.

When he did so, he came to see that what he felt was not just hurt but also a good deal of anger. He felt that the action had been totally unjust. He had been implicitly promised the next promotion and his performance appraisals had all been very positive. These feelings of anger at his boss were not, however, primary for him. It was much easier for him to be angry at himself and this appeared to be the core of his depression. However, the resolution of these feelings required that he face directly the fact and validity of his anger at his boss. And this led directly to their focus on the question of forgiveness. As noted earlier, feelings of anger and sadness are often intermixed in response to disappointment and hurt experienced at the hands of others. Both must be faced if the feelings are to be resolved. Some people, such as Paul, can more comfortably accept the sadness than the anger. They use their depression to defend against the feelings of anger. Others find anger more acceptable than depression. They use the anger to defend against the depression. But both groups of people must face both sets of interrelated feelings.

Denial of anger is, unfortunately, particularly common among Christians who have often failed to recognize that it is not anger itself which is sinful but rather the expression of those feelings which is either sinful or God-honoring. In order to clarify this matter, the pastor is often in a position where it is necessary to validate the feelings of anger. The person who has been hurt by the behavior of someone else needs to understand that anger is an appropriate response to such treatment. Anger is a natural response to injustice. This reaction was built into the fabric of our humanity and is a response that is shared with God. But as with every other aspect of the created order (including human personality), anger was affected by the fall and its expression easily reflects a desire for retaliation, not a desire for resolution of the injustice. If people fail to understand this distinction, or worse, if they believe that anger is in itself sinful, they will seek to eliminate the anger from their awareness. However, in so doing they will be hindered in their movement toward any genuine release of that anger.

The goal of Strategic Pastoral Counseling is not the expression of anger but rather the release of anger. Letting out anger should not be confused with, and is an extremely poor substitute for, letting go of anger. Ultimately, this release of anger is only possible through forgiveness. However, as noted, the process of forgiveness requires honestly dealing with the underlying feelings of both anger and hurt. Only when they are brought to the light of conscious awareness and examined for what they are and what they reveal about the nature of the underlying disappointment, can the hurt associated with that disappointment be genuinely healed.[1]

Disappointment with Self

But sometimes pastors encounter people whose disappointment seems more focused on themselves. Forgiveness may be a word that springs very readily to their lips as they proclaim their inability to forgive themselves. How are we to understand such problems and what is the Strategic Pastoral Counseling response to such individuals?

At first glance, this may appear to be a simpler problem to work with because the issue of forgiveness is so readily brought into the discussion. But any pastor who has counseled such individuals knows that there is often nothing simple about such work. Forgiveness of one's self is frequently at least as difficult as forgiveness of another and the fact that the discussion moves to the issue of forgiveness much quicker is often a very misleading indication of counseling progress.

There are, of course, times when the person who is having a hard time forgiving himself or herself simply needs to encounter the life transforming grace of God and receive his forgiveness. Self-forgiveness frequently follows naturally after the receipt of divine forgiveness. This is the way in which the process should work, and the fact that it does not always do so should not confuse us about the norm.

But the fact is that some people do not want to receive forgiveness—not from God, not from others, and not from themselves. Such individuals may come to the pastor for help with theological questions about forgiveness or the nature of God's love. More often, though, they come as the spouse of someone wanting marital help. Regardless of the way in which they come for pastoral help, the challenge is to avoid trying to convince them to accept God's forgiveness. Instead, the focus must be on why this forgiveness is so resisted.

In counseling which is initially focused on an experience of hurt at the hand of another, the challenge is to move from a focus on the other person to a focus on how that experience impacted the counselee. In contrast to this, the challenge in working with someone who states that they are unable to forgive themselves is to move beyond a focus on their symptoms of self-loathing or shame to an examination of the deeper source of their woundedness. Being stuck in feelings of shame is usually an indication that the counselee is nursing an injury to their core sense of self. In more technical language, this is often referred to as a narcissistic injury, an experience that leaves the person feeling worthless or defective in some basic and pervasive way. Such feelings of profound worthlessness are not readily changed. Change is, however, possible when the feelings are given full expression and the person is able to receive the acceptance and validation of their being from God, mediated through the acceptance and validation of their being offered by the pastor. While superficially it may appear that they need forgiveness for some unconfessed and awful sin, more commonly such people need repair to the basic sense of worth, something that comes from unconditional acceptance of them by the pastor.[2]

To illustrate the way in which a Strategic Pastoral Counselor could deal with problems with self-forgiveness, consider the following case. Sue was a quiet and rather introverted young woman in her early twenties who had recently married. She consulted her pastor at this point because she felt she had committed the unforgivable sin. Tearfully and with great effort, she told him that on a recent occasion of lovemaking with her husband she had found herself thinking about an old boyfriend. This was not the first time her pastor had dealt with Sue around the question of whether or not she had committed some sin which placed her beyond the pale of God's forgiveness. As a teen, she had consulted him with extreme pangs of guilt over feelings of resentment in relation to her father. At that point, it had been her pastor's judgment that her feelings were not an expression of sorrow over sin, but were instead the result of a neurotic and distorted conscience which tyrannized her and resulted in her feelings of self-loathing. His immediate inclination was to view the present situation in the same light.

Exploration of her concern was, however, the appropriate beginning point and he asked her to tell him more about what she felt she had done that was so awful that it placed her outside of God's grace. What she reported was a fleeting image of this other male, something very different than a nurtured fantasy of lust. He made this distinction for her but it proved quite unhelpful. It was her firm conviction that this was lust of the worst kind and that she no longer deserved either the love of her husband or of her God.

Sue's problems were quite deep and were not something which could be resolved in a few sessions of pastoral counseling. However, the pastor wisely recognized that while she needed a referral to a mental health counselor for more long-term psychological help, there were very unique pastoral responses which he could offer her which would go beyond merely trying to convince her to accept God's forgiveness.

After approximately twenty minutes of discussion about these matters, the pastor indicated that he had some ideas about how he felt he could best help her. He first suggested a referral to a Christian counselor who was well-known to him and explained to Sue why he thought that this was important. He told her that if she were to accept this suggestion, he would then be better able to help her in some uniquely pastoral ways, something that he very much hoped he could do. Somewhat reluctantly she agreed and he then laid out for her his proposal.

His suggestion was that she first commit herself to an in-depth study of the concepts of divine love and grace as revealed in the

Bible. He suggested some beginning points for this study, but knowing her to be quite capable of using biblical reference tools, he suggested that she follow these up with the leads which her own
research suggested. He then asked that she keep a record of both
her discoveries in this research and of her reactions to those discoveries. Their meeting times, which he scheduled once per month,
would consist of her reporting both her discoveries and reactions,
and their discussion of the same. Once again, her agreement was
reluctant. She said she was already sufficiently familiar with the
Christian understanding of grace. What she was more interested
in studying was God's justice and his punishment of sin. She did,
however, accept the assignment as it formed the condition for his
being willing to talk with her further about why she deserved God's
punishment, not his love.

The pastor's plan was to first focus more on her reactions to what
she learned, only briefly reviewing the actual principles she was
discovering. This would give her the opportunity to explore why
she resisted God's forgiveness and would also allow them together
to deal with other issues which might emerge from her work with
the Christian counselor.

As anticipated, Sue's reaction to the first four weeks of study
was one of resistance to divine grace. She protested that if God
really loved her, he would recognize her need for punishment and
honor this. His failure to punish her was a flaw in his love. She then
disclosed a fact that had recently first been shared with her other
counselor, namely that she had been abused as a child by a grandmother who did so while constantly assuring her that the beatings
were for her good and were because the grandmother loved her.
The sadistic nature of her grandmother's long-standing treatment
of Sue had caused immense damage to her basic sense of worth
and this appeared to be at the core of her problems.

The course of the subsequent pastoral counseling sessions followed the pattern of allowing Sue to first report what she had
uncovered from her research and then share her reactions to this.
Ever so slowly, the emphasis of the sessions began to shift and the
focus came to be more and more that of Sue's discoveries about
God's nature. In the fourth session, she acknowledged that previously she had never really allowed herself to experience God's for-

giveness, and had done this in the weeks since the last session. She also gave clear evidence of beginning to feel better about herself.

In the fifth session, the pastor indicated that he felt it was no longer necessary for them to meet regularly. Sue said that she felt fine about this as long as she could come back from time to time to discuss her continuing progress on these matters. Asking her what she had found most helpful about their sessions together, she indicated that it was unquestionably his acceptance of her. The pastor at first found this a little disconcerting, expecting that surely it had been some of the theological insights he had shared with her. Her experience, however, was one of having been assured of her worth by his willingness to wade with her through the muck of her self-loathing. She told him that God's love for her had only begun to make sense as she came to understand and appreciate the love she had been receiving from him.

This case study, based on a counseling relationship with an actual person, may seem too good to be true. For, as acknowledged, the sort of damage to self-worth that profound self-loathing and shame reveal is something which typically is changed only slowly and with great difficulty. However, the point of the illustration is that difficulties in both self-forgiveness or in the receipt of divine forgiveness usually require a response to the reasons for the resistance to forgiveness. This, in turn, usually involves an exploration of the way in which the person's worth was damaged and, as was the case with Sue, this very frequently involves childhood abuse.

In such cases, the discussion of forgiveness has come full circle because now, once again, we have a situation wherein the person must be willing to forgive someone who hurt them if they are to be free of the unwanted side effects of this trauma. Problems in self-forgiveness or in the receipt of divine forgiveness are seen to often be, therefore, disguised problems in forgiving someone who has hurt them.

Disappointment with God

The fact that life is often unfair leads many people to conclude that God is unfair. Often these people are within the church and, consequently, they are frequently encountered by pastors who counsel. How should a pastor respond to an assertion about the unfairness of God? Although the feeling of disappointment with God may correspond to the feeling of being disappointed by another human, it does raise some important questions. Is it appropriate to be angry at God? Is it meaningful to speak of forgiving God? And perhaps basic of all, where is God when people experience the obvious unfairness of life?

In his book *Disappointment with God,* Philip Yancey suggests that the feelings of anger at God reflect a confusion of God and life. There is no question, he suggests, that life is unfair. Children are physically and sexually abused, earthquakes destroy life and property, and loved ones are killed or injured by hit and run drunk drivers. But where is God when these things happen? Yancey's answer is that God is in us as we experience these injustices—not in the abusers, earthquakes, and hit and run drivers. God is not behind these disasters in life. Rather he stands with us, sharing our anger, hurt, despair, and pain.[3]

While this answer to the question of God's responsibility for human suffering may not solve all the theological issues that are involved, it does seem to provide the framework for an appropriate and helpful pastoral care response to the problem. But it is also important to realize that an expression of anger at God for his unfairness or lack of care is usually less a theological assertion than an emotional expression. God's reputation does not require the protection that we may think we can afford by a sturdy rebuttal of the theological errors of such an assertion, at least not as a first response. While a discussion of the theological aspects of the question may be appropriate at a later point, usually the most fitting first response is to encourage the person to tell more of their story. Their statement about God is merely part of the conclusion to their story. What the pastoral counselor needs to hear is how they came to this conclusion.

Disappointments with God should, therefore, be treated as any other disappointment. The pastor should encourage the person to explore and express the feelings and describe the events associated with them. Defensiveness regarding the expression of anger at God on the part of the pastor will undoubtedly be quickly picked up by the counselee and will impede this exploration. For this reason, the pastor may find it helpful to make a brief statement of his or her own feelings about God's responsibility for the events of the person's life if this helps reduce such defensiveness. This should then be followed by encouraging the person to continue to express their feelings.

Properly understood, it makes no sense, whatsoever, to speak of forgiving God. Such a notion completely distorts the concept of forgiveness. It may be appropriate to forgive someone who hasn't sought my forgiveness or even someone who does not desire it. But it only makes sense to speak of offering my forgiveness to someone who needs it. God does not ever need our forgiveness. Such a notion is blasphemous. It should, however, be treated in a different manner in a counseling session than in grading a paper from a seminarian in a graduate course in theology. In counseling, it should be redirected by something like, "While I understand your anger at God, I am not sure that it really makes any sense to speak of your offering him your forgiveness. But let's continue to look at just why you are so angry at him."

Forgiveness Counseling

Helping people deal redemptively with experiences of abuse, betrayal, rejection, and disappointment can at the same time be one of the most demanding and rewarding aspects of pastoral care. While the difficulties of such work should not be minimized, neither should the rewards.

Helping others receive healing of the spiritual and psychological damage associated with such experiences requires that the pastoral counselor take into his or her own person the pain, hurt, terror, and shame born by the counselee. These feelings cannot be merely discussed. They must be shared. This was what Sue was referring to when she indicated that the most helpful aspect of her counseling with her pastor had been his acceptance of her. This empathic acceptance of the feelings of the counselee is extremely demanding on the psychospiritual resources of the pastor. As the pastor temporarily takes into his or her person the anger, fear, mistrust, and other negative feelings associated with the emotional injury, he or she experiences much of the same depletion of well-being that the counselee is describing. This is true sharing of one another's burdens. It can't be done from the sidelines and it is always personally costly.

One of these costs is that such experiences may resurrect for the pastor unresolved matters from his or her own past. Feelings which may have been judged to be long ago dealt with may suddenly be re-awakened, and people assumed to have been already forgiven may again have to be mentally faced with fresh offerings of forgiveness. Only when the pastor is able to honestly face whatever feelings are encountered is he or she able to assist the counselee in doing the same.

But dealing with experiences of undeserved hurt also offers unique opportunities to witness the redemptive power of the gospel firsthand and up close. This is one of the great rewards to the counselor dealing with those who seek help for emotional wounds. People do not have to be the victims of their past. This good news is very much a part of the Good News, the gospel. The undeserved hurts and injustices which people experience can be redeemed and out of ashes can come a garland of praise.

Forgiveness is never simply a Band-aid to be placed over emotional injury. Real forgiveness is hard work and always involves honestly dealing with all the feelings that are involved. Real forgiveness of significant wounds is also seldom a one-time affair. It is offered as a part of a process and most often it must be offered over and over again. It is never a shortcut to counseling. But it is an indispensable part of any counseling that genuinely resolves past hurts. Furthermore, it is a foundational aspect of any counseling that seeks to be distinctively Christian.

Stages and Tasks of Forgiveness Counseling

The general pattern of Strategic Pastoral Counseling focused around questions of forgiveness is presented in overview fashion in the preface and described in more detail in the first volume of this series (*Strategic Pastoral Counseling* by David G. Benner, 1992). By way of brief review and as a reminder of the framework which will structure the case presentations in the next three chapters, Table 1 presents the stages and tasks of Strategic Pastoral Counseling.

Table 1

Stages and Tasks of Strategic Pastoral Counseling

Stage 1: Encounter
* Joining and boundary setting
* Exploring the central concerns and relevant history
* Conducting a pastoral diagnosis
* Achieving a mutually agreeable focus for counseling

Stage 2: Engagement
* Exploration of cognitive, affective, and behavioral aspects
  of problem and the identification of resources for coping or change

Stage 3: Disengagement
* Evaluation of progress and assessment of remaining concerns
* Referral (if needed)
* Termination of counseling

The encounter stage normally occupies most of the first session, subsequent sessions being spent primarily on engagement stage tasks and, more briefly, disengagement tasks. However, the flow of these stages of Strategic Pastoral Counseling is not always linear and there is no assumption that work on one stage cannot occur at the same time as work on another. There is, also, no assumption that a full five sessions must be taken with every counselee. In some cases, a single session allows the pastor to accomplish the work of each of the above stages.

6

Case Study I*

Karen is a twenty-six-year-old woman who contacted her pastor by phone and asked if she could come to see him. Her pastor knew her only slightly, she and her husband having first come to his congregation approximately one year earlier, but since then only attending services sporadically. He recalled that she was a nurse, that her husband worked in advertising, and that they had no children. He had also been aware that in the past several months, when Karen was in church she was there alone. He had intended to give her a call to see if everything was alright but had not done so before receiving her phone call.

In this phone call, Karen gave little indication of why she wished to see the pastor other than that, in her words, she "was having a hard time coping with some changes in her life." The pastor asked

---

*The best way to present some of the strategies and approaches to pastoral care situations involving forgiveness is by means of a case study. This and the next three chapters will, therefore, each examine one case of a person seen by a pastor for a short-term counseling experience that focuses on questions of forgiveness. These cases, while hypothetical (in order to preserve confidentiality), are each a composite of a number of people seen by the authors.

101

her if she needed to see him right away and she indicated that, while the matter was not urgent, she would be glad if he could see her as soon as possible. He stated that he had an hour available the next morning and that if this time was convenient for her he would look forward to meeting with her and hearing more about her concerns. She agreed to the time and thanked him for being willing to see her so soon.

Commentary: This short interaction accomplished the major objective of a first contact in that it allowed the pastor to make a judgement about the urgency of the situation and set a time for the first appointment. While Karen told him that her need to see him was not urgent, she also expressed her hope that she could see him soon. Thus, he concluded that while this was not an emergency, it was important enough that he should see her the next day. Her appreciation for such an immediate appointment seemed to confirm the correctness of his judgement.

Not always will the first contact indicate the nature of the concerns of the person seeking help. In the present situation, the pastor approached the first session knowing that the reason she wished to talk with him had something to do with recent changes in her life. He did not know what these changes were, nor was there any need for him to know more at this point. Wisely, he refrained from asking her further about this on the phone. At this point it is not usually appropriate to ask questions about the nature of these concerns, nor is it profitable to encourage the person to talk further about them. In fact, it is often appropriate to say to the parishioner who begins to get into the details of his or her problems that there is no need to say more now, but that he will look forward to hearing about these matters in detail at the first session. Someone in crisis is obviously an exception to this general principle.

First Session

Karen arrived at the pastor's office the next morning looking tired and somewhat distressed. The pastor noticed immediately that she had lost some weight since he had last seen her. She also looked as if she had just been crying. The following interaction ensued:

Pastor: Good morning Karen. I'm glad to see that you made it. Why don't you come right on into my office. (They enter together and he points to a chair where she can sit.) I gathered from our brief conversation yesterday that you were facing some changes in your life and were concerned about how well you were coping with them. Would you like to tell me more about these concerns?

Karen: Thank you for seeing me so soon. I really feel silly coming to see you but I just don't know who else to talk to. (beginning to cry) Ken left me for another woman and I'm just so confused and upset. I can't believe this is happening to me. (long pause)

Pastor: I am really sorry to hear that news. I don't doubt for a minute that you have found this upsetting. It must feel like the bottom has fallen out of your world.

Karen: That's just exactly what it feels like. It came as such a surprise. I thought things were going alright between us. And then this. Wham! Out of the blue he tells me one morning that he has decided to leave me. Then he walked out of the door for work and I haven't seen him since.

Pastor: When did this happen?

Karen: Last Monday. He was away for several days last week and weekend, traveling for work, or at least that is what he told me. He came home late Sunday night and everything seemed okay, although we didn't talk much. And then Monday morning he made his announcement and was gone before I knew what had hit me.

Commentary: This is a good beginning for a first session. The pastor gets right down to business without a lot of unnecessary small talk. This worked fine with Karen although sometimes a bit more social interaction is appropriate and necessary. Seldom, however, should such small talk occupy more than a couple of minutes. The task of this first stage of Strategic Pastoral Counseling is joining, that is, the establishment of a sufficient connection that the parishioner feels free to proceed with the telling of his or her story. The pastor in the present situation judged this connection to be present immediately and correctly concluded, therefore, that no casual conversation was necessary.

The pastor also did a good job of briefly indicating what he recalled of their previous conversation. This served to let Karen know that he had been listening and also provided a good initial focus for their conversation.

His second statement demonstrates a high level of empathy and her response shows how powerful such an intervention can be in facilitating further exploration. Empathy communicates back to the person an understanding of what has been communicated thus far and in this case, the pastor did this by picking up on her use of the word "upset" and elaborating by means of a metaphor (the bottom falling out of her world). Word pictures such as this are often very powerful ways of reflecting back the feelings that are being heard and doing so in a way that encourages further exploration of the matter under discussion.

But at this point, the pastor wants both feelings and context and for this reason he then asks a very specific question ("When did this happen?"). The pastor is now beginning the second task of the Encounter stage, namely, the exploration of the parishioner's central concerns and relevant history. Details are important in this stage. Feelings should be attached to specific events in order to ensure the level of concreteness and specificity that is necessary for a short-term counseling relationship. The pastor then continues with a question designed to further explore the background to her central concern.

Pastor: You say that everything seemed pretty normal when your husband came home on Sunday. Tell me a bit more about how things had been between the two of you recently.

Karen: Well, normal wasn't really all that good. Ken and I never talked with each other very much, at least not about important things. That has always bothered me but whenever I tried to talk with him about my feelings he would get furious and we would have a fight.

Pastor: Did you fight a lot?

Karen: Not at first, but in the last year or so we seemed to get into fights all the time.

Pastor: You say things were better at first. Tell me a bit about that period of your marriage.

Commentary: Once again, what the pastor is attempting to do here is get some context for the present problems. Her present feelings will need further exploration in this session but a brief review of the history of the marriage will help the pastor put these feelings into the context of Karen's marriage and life.

Karen then proceeded to tell the pastor about her courtship with Ken and their early years of marriage. They had met at university through a campus Christian fellowship and had three good years before they married. During this period Ken showed occasional problems controlling his temper but Karen had minimized the significance of this. He also showed hints of what would later be seen as a tendency to emotional abuse, criticizing her maliciously but always following this with apologies and acts of contrition.

Marriage seemed, however, to change everything. Immediately after their marriage Ken seemed to lose interest in his wife. Karen reported that he also seemed to lose interest in his faith. His attendance at church decreased and his criticism of anything to do with religion increased. In general, he became more sarcastic and cynical and Karen often wondered what had happened to change him in such a major way. At this point, the pastor shifted the direction of the session, returning Karen to further discussion of her present feelings.

Pastor: That's very helpful background and we may return to it later. But let's go back now to where you started when you first came in. You said that you were feeling confused and upset. Tell me more about how you have coped since last Monday.

Karen: Well at first I just cried. In fact, I cried most of that day. But I kept hoping that it wasn't true and that he would come home after work. That first night was awful. I hardly slept at all. All I could think about was how badly I wanted him to come back. But by the next day that began to change. I still wanted him back but I started to get really angry at him. That was when it started to sink in that he had left me for another woman. He wouldn't tell me anything about her but I started to hate her. And him. Every time I thought of him I saw some young thing with him and that made me furious.

Pastor: You said you didn't know who else to talk with about this. Have you told your family or any close friends about Ken's leaving?

Commentary: This question is a very important one. Here the pastor is trying to assess how Karen is coping and what resources, beyond himself, are available to her. Strategic Pastoral Counseling can only work as a short-term counseling experience when the pastor works alongside of others who are available to, or already involved in helping roles with, the parishioner. Identifying the resources which are available to the counselee is, therefore, an important part of the first session.

Exploration of the counselee's present coping is also an important part of assessment that is necessary in order to plan future sessions. At this point the pastor is wondering how depressed she is and how badly her coping has been affected by the events they have been discussing. Has she pulled back from her friends? How well has she coped with her other responsibilities? Is she hanging on by her fingernails or is her grasp of her life situation more firm? These are the sorts of questions that lay behind his request for information about who else she had talked with.

In response to this question, Karen stated that she had called her mother on Tuesday night and that she had been a big support. Her mother asked her to come and stay with her for a few days and she had been living there for the past ten days. Since then she had told a couple of their closest friends, although she hadn't seen any of these people yet. She was scheduled to have lunch with one of these friends the next day but was nervous about this since this friend had been close to both her and Ken since before they were married. The pastor encouraged her to keep this lunch appointment.

He then asked her whether her faith had been of any help through this crisis. She reported that she hadn't really thought about her faith, or of God, for that matter, since Ken had left. This question was followed by several others designed to provide an assessment of her religious and spiritual functioning.

Pastor: I hope my asking whether your faith was a resource for you didn't appear too preachy. I really am not trying to lay a guilt trip on you but just to get a sense of where you are spiritually.

Karen: No, it didn't seem too preachy and I'm glad that you asked. That is one of the things I hoped to talk with you about. My faith is very important to me but I just don't know what difference it should make to me now. I suppose I should be praying about all the things that have happened but I don't really know what to pray, whether to pray that Ken will come back or stay away.

Pastor: How about praying that God will help you cope with the mixed-up feelings you are facing? Does that seem like something that he could or would do?

Karen: Well I suppose so but I'm actually a little ashamed of my feelings. I guess I feel that I should get my act together before I bother God with all this stuff. I mean it seems pretty funny to pray to God for help with my feelings of hate for Ken. After all, I shouldn't be feeling hate.

Pastor: I wouldn't be so quick to say that you shouldn't be feeling whatever you are feeling. It seems to me that what your husband has done to you makes strong feelings pretty natural. Hate isn't a very nice feeling and it surely isn't something that anyone should hold onto a minute longer than is necessary. But it's my experience that strong feelings of anger and rage usually accompany a significant emotional wound. Healing of the wound you have experienced will require facing the feelings, not trying to convince yourself that they are not there.

Karen: I guess that's true but where does God fit into all of that?

Pastor: I believe that God's place in a situation like this is right beside you, so close, in fact, that he shares your anger and pain and wants you to know that his grace is sufficient for you in the midst of these awful experiences.

Karen: (Crying) I wish I could believe that. I want to. I need to know that God is still there and that he hasn't left me too. I guess I just feel so ugly and unloveable that I can't believe that anyone still loves me, especially God.

Pastor: Why especially God? Why is his love especially hard to believe in or count on?

Karen: I guess because I know how high his standards are.

Pastor: That's certainly true and it is clear that you don't want to min-imize his hatred of sin. But I wonder if you haven't lost sight of another thing that is equally true about God and that is the extravagance of his love and the consistency of his grace. You seem to see him as somewhat miserly with his love, dish-ing it out in small doses to people who deserve it. But the God I know through Scriptures is a God who lavishes his love on sinners who do nothing to deserve it. That's a quality of God that I hope you can come to know more personally.

At this point the pastor thought that he had a relatively good sense of her spiritual functioning and, noticing that they had been talking for forty-five minutes, decided to move discussion toward a contract for future work together and bring the session to a close. This led to the following interchange.

Pastor: Our time is just about up for this morning and I am wonder-ing how you feel about what has happened in our time together.

Karen: I feel quite a bit better and am really glad that I came to see you. I still feel awfully upset but it helps to talk about it.

Pastor: I certainly wouldn't expect you to feel all better so quickly but I am glad that you feel a bit better. I wonder if you feel that you got what you came for or if you would like to talk about these matters some more another day.

Karen: I hope that we can talk again. I found this really helpful but there is still so much that confuses me.

Pastor: Perhaps that is where we could begin the next time, with those feelings of confusion. My recommendation is that we meet for a couple of times, perhaps up to a maximum of four more ses-sions. Let's space these out in whatever way makes the most sense to us and we can review how things are going for you each time we get together. How does that sound to you?

Karen: That sounds good. I look forward to seeing you again when-ever you think is best.

Pastor: Why don't we make the next meeting two weeks from today? This will give you a chance to think further about some of the things we have discussed. I'd also like to suggest that you keep track of what you are feeling and thinking, perhaps in a journal or some way of keeping a record of your reflections and feelings. That should help us as we go to work the next time trying to make some sense of the feelings that you are finding so confusing.

Karen: That sounds fine. I do write in a journal occasionally and could easily do so more regularly.

Pastor: There is one more thing I'd like you to do between now and when we next meet. I'd like to ask you to reflect further on God's love for you. Take a look at a couple of passages that I will jot down for you in a minute and reflect on what they mean for you. I believe they will offer you some comfort and hope, and that they will help you experience the presence of God with you in the midst of your present situation.

Commentary: In this session most of the tasks of the Encounter stage of Strategic Pastoral Counseling were accomplished. The pastor has explored the central concerns and relevant history, conducted a brief spiritual assessment, and achieved an agreed upon focus for future work together.

The only aspect of this session which might be faulted is with regard to this focus for future work. Karen and the pastor agreed that the next session would be used to further explore the confusing feelings she was facing. In his own mind, the pastor had thought he had identified feelings of loss and sadness as well as feelings of anger. Thus, the tentative plan which he had in mind was one wherein they would explore these feelings and move toward her forgiveness of her husband. He anticipated that this work might also involve them in some discussion of practical matters related to the separation and he was also prepared to do this. However, none of this was explicitly discussed between them. Their explicit contract for work really only involved the next session. While it might have been difficult to spell out specifically what their focus would be after this first session, some consideration of the bigger goals Karen hoped to accomplish by their work together would have been helpful. This would have also allowed the pastor to share some of his implicit goals and expectations.

Second Session

Two weeks later Karen arrived at her appointment looking considerably better. Opening conversation went as follows:

Karen: I have been really looking forward to coming to see you today. I can't tell you how much better I feel since we last talked.

Pastor: I am delighted to hear that. Often it does seem to help just to share one's feelings with someone else. But tell me why you were looking forward to coming again today.

Karen: Well, the things you told me to think about were really helpful. You suggested that I keep track of what I was feeling. I did this and what I discovered was that I was really angry. I told you that I was meeting with a girlfriend the day after I saw you and she helped me a lot too. She told me to forget Ken, that he wasn't worthy of me, and that I shouldn't take him back even if he came begging for forgiveness. The more I thought about him, the more furious I became with him. I still haven't seen him and I don't care if I ever see him again. The way he treated me, he could go to hell for all I care.

Commentary: The pastor was more than a little surprised by the dramatic change in Karen and began to wonder if he had overdone the legitimization of anger in the last session. Karen was behaving in a more assertive manner and there was no sign of tears being close to the surface as had been the case in the previous session. In fact, if he could have admitted it to himself, he was somewhat taken aback by her anger. The strength of her feelings made him somewhat uncomfortable. Let's examine two possible ways in which he could respond to these feelings and probable ways in which Karen might respond.

Pastor: Well, I wouldn't want to go that far. To damn someone to hell is pretty serious business. That's business that really should be left to God.

Karen: I guess I don't really mean that I want him to go to hell. That's just how I feel. But I thought you said that anger was okay.

Commentary: This would be an unfortunate intervention on the part of the pastor as his defensiveness would now be shared by Karen. If he had been able to take the statement about hell as an indication of the strength of her anger and not been drawn into dealing with it as a theological assertion, both of them would have been spared this distraction. As it was, he would now have to back up and try to restate his position in a way that legitimized anger but qualified its means of appropriate expression. Even though the content of this statement would be important, its timing would be most unfortunate. After this interchange, Karen would likely be somewhat more careful about how she expressed herself. Sadly, she would have learned that raw feelings are not appropriate for sharing with the pastor and, henceforth, she would probably resolve to package them in a somewhat nicer manner before putting them on the table.

The way in which feelings are expressed is, of course, very important. However, at this point in the counseling relationship, the goal is to discover just what feelings are actually present. They must first be taken as they are if they are to be subsequently modified. The message Karen would have heard from this encounter would be that if certain feelings are offensive, they should be hidden. This is a very poor substitute for transformation which always starts with an honest acceptance of reality.

Consider now what the pastor actually said and note the difference in Karen's response.

Pastor: You really are feeling awfully angry at Ken. It sounds like you couldn't imagine a fate that would be worse than what he deserves.

Karen: That's exactly what I am feeling! I mean, he's just scum. To walk out on me for no reason other than that he found some young chick who excited him more than me makes him the lowest of the low. I mean, I just can't imagine how he could do that to me. He obviously has been lying to me for months. He has been seeing this other woman while he was still living with me and that really hurts. That just makes me want to scream. (Starting to cry) It just makes me furious.

Pastor: It makes you furious but it also brings a lot of pain. And I understand that. He has hurt you very badly. What you are feeling is both the open wound of that hurt and anger in response to it.

Karen: That's so true. I wish I could just feel anger at him. But that is only half of what I feel. The other half is just like you say, its pain. It feels like someone stabbed me in my stomach and twisted the knife. And it hurts! It hurts really bad! (More crying) It hurts worse than I've ever hurt before. And I don't know if I can stand it.

Pastor: That's where the anger comes in. I suspect it is serving to protect you from some of the pain you are feeling. Both the anger and the pain are natural consequences of the hurt you have experienced. Sometimes the anger will be easier to face than the pain and sometimes the pain might be closer to the surface. We will have to look at both sets of feelings and I'm glad that you have been able to identify both in your reactions this past couple of weeks.

Commentary: This was a very nice interchange and the pastor's willingness to stay with Karen's strong feelings allowed her to do the same and then to begin to see beyond them. The pastor's last response serves an educative function of informing Karen in terms of what their subsequent work together will involve. This isn't the last time they will look at the connection of the anger and the pain but this brief statement will help Karen bring intellectual resources into her response to her pain. Working through the consequences of her emotional injury will require dealing with the emotional, intellectual, and behavioral components of the situation. This intervention helps connect the emotional and the intellectual components.

At this point Karen began to talk more about the hurt which she was feeling and expressed how devastated she had felt when Ken first walked out on her. Throughout this discussion, anger and sadness were intermixed. This discussion indicated that much of Karen's anger at her husband predated his leaving her and was associated with a long-standing pattern of verbal and emotional abuse. This led to the following interchange:

Karen: Like I told you last time, Ken had an incredible ability to hurt with words. When he would get mad he would say the most cruel things. He would tell me things like, that I didn't have a brain in my head, or, that even my friends must laugh at me behind my back because I was so ridiculously stupid. Sometimes I could ignore this because I used to feel reasonably good about myself. But when he kept saying things like this I started to believe it. I just hate him for that. He is so cruel.

Pastor: You did mention the way he treated you the last time and I think it is important that we now talk further about that. The more I listen to you, the more I sense that your hurt and anger goes back much farther than the past couple of weeks. You are not just dealing with feelings about his having left you. You are dealing with feelings associated with years' worth of emotional abuse.

Commentary: The pastor was about to follow this last sentence with a statement regarding the importance of dealing with these feelings from the past if she was to be able to forgive her husband, but stopped in the face of some uncertainty about how to introduce the concept of forgiveness. He had been thinking about forgiveness ever since the first session and felt strongly that this was a goal toward which Karen should be moving. However, he was sensitive to the fact that the timing of the introduction of this concept was crucial.

He was quite correct in this sensitivity and his last minute judgement that this was not the correct time seems well-founded. There is no question that for the ultimate healing of the emotional wounds caused by her husband, Karen would have to release her anger at him in an act (or, more likely, a series of acts) of forgiveness. But in order to be ready to do this, she would first have to know what it was for which she had to forgive him. Forgiveness offered at this point would either be premature or, at the least, partial. Real and meaningful forgiveness is an act of the will in which anger is released and relinquished. But before that can be done, the anger and the associated hurts must be known. In Karen's case, this work was still in its infancy.

Karen now proceeded to explore and express the feelings associated with the long-standing emotional abuse which she had received from her husband. This was very difficult for her as she had never previously told anyone about this. As is often the case, her response to this abuse was a deep sense of shame. She felt hurt and angry, but she felt that somehow she must deserve the treatment he had given her. Tragically, and significantly, she had been the victim of such abuse in several relationships with males. Wondering if this pattern had begun with abuse by her father, the pastor asked this question directly. Karen denied that he had ever abused her in any way.

Commentary: This direct inquiry about the possibility of abuse in her family of origin was highly appropriate. With what we now know about the very high incidence of physical, sexual, and emotional abuse in families, whenever there is any reason whatsoever to suspect it, the matter should be directly queried. Pastoral counselors must be able to ask this question. To fail to do so, out of either personal discomfort or a false belief that abuse does not happen within the church, is nothing less than an abdication of one's professional responsibilities as a pastoral counselor. Many people who have actually been the victims of abuse will deny that fact when first asked. However, a large percentage will acknowledge their abuse and this will always have important implications for counseling.

After adding feelings of shame to the already identified feelings of anger and pain, Karen stated that the good feelings with which she had come to this session were now pretty much gone. This gave the pastor another chance to interpret the feelings of anger which were dominant in the first part of this session as defenses against these deeper and more distressing feelings. Karen then expressed that in many ways she would prefer the anger and asked what was so bad about that. This led to the following interaction:

Pastor: I think I can understand that you might prefer the feelings of anger. I think most of us do. Not only does it hold at bay some of the other more unpleasant feelings, it also tends to give us a sense of power. I think I sensed that in you when you first came in today. The last time I saw you, you looked totally defeated but when you came in today you seemed, well, more powerful—less defeated.

Commentary: Karen had asked the pastor what was so wrong with anger and he wisely chose to ignore this question. Instead, he responded to her statement that she preferred the anger to the pain. This was a good choice. Instead of trying to talk her into relinquishing her anger, his strategy was to help her come to the point where she understood both the payoffs and costs of her anger and was, herself, ready to let go of it. This explains the pastor's paradoxical response to her question. Karen asked him what was so bad about anger. His response was to help her see some of the advantages of the anger (i.e., her increased sense of personal power). Ignoring or minimizing the payoffs of undesirable behaviors or feelings such as anger only serves to minimize the chances of any real change.

Karen: Actually, that's true. That was one of the ways my girlfriend helped me. She helped me see that I deserved to be angry and that felt a lot better. But actually, I'm not really sure that I want to be angry, at least not for the rest of my life. My girlfriend is. I mean she just seems to have a chip on her shoulder. And the chip is men. She has become a real man-hater since her marriage broke up. She doesn't date or even relate to men anymore. I guess I don't really want to be like that. I don't just mean about hating men. I mean I don't really want to hate.

Pastor: Why not? Let me ask you the question you asked me. What's so wrong with anger?

Karen: Well, I just don't really like the angry people I know. They aren't nice to be around. And I don't want to be like that. Besides, I know that Christianity teaches that anger is bad. I know you said something about that the last time and I'm not really sure I understood. But I know that we are supposed to love our enemies, not hate them.

Pastor: Well, whatever I said and whatever you caught or didn't catch, you certainly have the most important aspect of the

Christian teaching on anger and that is that in Christ we have an alternative to being stuck in our feelings of anger. That alternative is forgiveness of those who hurt us. Without the possibility of forgiveness, we would be victims of our past, victims of the unfair things that happen to us. But while forgiveness is difficult, in fact, it is probably the most difficult thing a person can ever be asked to do, in Christ it is possible and it is the only route to healing of emotional wounds such as you have received that I know.

Karen: I guess I believe that but I'm not sure that I want to forgive Ken. Does that sound really awful?

Pastor: In fact it doesn't. It sounds pretty realistic. If you had told me that you were ready to forgive him, I would have told you to take your time. Not that I want you to hold onto your anger a minute longer than you have to, but I do believe that you must be ready to forgive a person who has hurt you. Forgiveness of big hurts such as you have experienced is a process. You have to know what it is that you need to forgive him for and to know that you need to know your feelings. What you are now discovering is that knowing your feelings takes a bit of time. Two weeks ago you knew that Ken hurt you by walking out on you. But today we have also discovered that he has hurt you in a great many more ways and over a much longer period of time. There is actually quite a bit that you will ultimately be called upon to forgive him for. And you will probably have to do it in bits and pieces.

Commentary: Forgiveness was now on the table. But it was there because Karen was ready to begin looking at it. By her own admission, she was well aware that this was part of her duty as a Christian. Most Christians are. But what she was now learning was not simply the theoretical importance of forgiveness in the Christian life but the practical process of forgiveness of her husband whose abuse, unfaithfulness, and abandonment of her was still only beginning to be acknowledged.

Realizing that their time was almost up and that they had not yet discussed Karen's reactions to the reading assignment which he had given, he asked her now if she had managed to look up any of the passages he had given her. She replied that she had and that it had helped her sense God's love for her and his presence with her. She also reported that she had been more faithful in her prayers since their last session, still not knowing how to pray about Ken but praying regularly that God would help her pick up the pieces of her life and keep on going. The pastor suggested that she continue to read passages which would further assure her of these qualities of God, as the future might well bring more days when his presence would be difficult to discern. He indicated that he would give her some further passages at the end of the session. He also gave her a copy of *Choosing the Gift of Forgiveness*, the companion volume written to accompany this book but written for counselees, and suggested that she read as much of it as she could before the next session.

He then asked her to begin to write out a list of the things which Ken had done to hurt her and to prayerfully consider forgiving him of those wrongs for which she was ready. He asked her to bring this list to the next session and told her they would talk about the items on it which made forgiveness most difficult.

Finally, the pastor stated that while he had heard a good deal of her feelings, he wasn't hearing much about how she was coping with the absence of her husband. He indicated that this was something about which he would like to hear more when next they met. They then set this session for three weeks later and ended the present one with prayer.

Commentary: This second session focused primarily on an exploration of the affective aspects of Karen's problems and was quite productive. The three major feelings which were a part of her reaction to her husband had been identified and received some exploration. More work would need to be done on this but much of this could now be done by Karen alone.

The pastor's suggestion at the end of the session that they talk more the next time about how Karen was actually coping came as a result of suddenly realizing that he had heard very little about the external events of her life. He began to wonder if she was continuing to meet her work responsibilities, how she was relating

*to her family and friends, and what she was doing with her free
time. He hoped to deal with more of these concrete and behavioral
aspects of her life situation in the next session.*

Third Session

Karen began the next session, three weeks later, by informing
the pastor that she had heard from her husband and that he wanted
a divorce. He had written her a letter informing her of this fact and
suggested that she would be hearing from his attorney in the near
future. He also stated that he wanted to arrange a time when she
would be out of the house for him to return to clear out his remaining personal possessions.

The pastor's first response to this news was to ask Karen how
she felt about hearing from her husband. Not surprisingly, she had
been very upset. The letter had confronted her afresh with the reality of the termination of her marriage and she experienced a fresh
round of deep sadness and rage. She had begun to think about
things for which she needed to forgive Ken and this development
left her so angry that she abandoned this task, stating that she
wasn't ready to even think about forgiveness. The pastor indicated
understanding of this feeling and suggested that they put the matter of this list to one side until later and that they talk more about
how she wanted to deal with his request for a divorce and for a visit
to clear out his possessions.

*Commentary: This shift away from the mutually agreed upon
plan to use this session to talk about her "forgiveness list" was
obviously appropriate. Strategic Pastoral Counseling proceeds
in a planned manner but must always be responsive to unantic-
ipated developments such as occurred in this situation. However,
the pastor did not need to totally abandon his plan for this session. He had also decided that he wanted to deal with more of the
concrete aspects of her life situation and this development certainly gave him a good chance to do this. This was the reason
that he framed his suggestion about the use of the next part of
this session in terms of talking more about how she wanted to
deal with the development. Her feelings were something which*

he certainly was prepared to explore. However, he wanted to make the primary focus her behavior, that is, how she was coping and what she was going to do in response to the letter from her husband. He also hoped to be able to return to the question of forgiveness before the end of the session.

Karen indicated that she was totally confused about how to handle the situation she now faced. She had thought that she had given up all hope of salvaging the marriage, but now that she was faced with Ken's expressed desire for a divorce she suddenly realized that she was more ambivalent about the matter than she had thought. The pastor invited her to explore this ambivalence.

Karen: Well, on the one hand, I'm so furious with him that I couldn't divorce him fast enough. He really has his nerve. He cheated on me, walked out on me, and now, less than a month later, decides that a divorce will serve him best. Maybe that's exactly why I shouldn't give him one. (Pause) But, that would just be hurting myself. (Beginning to cry) And a divorce is hurting myself too, because I guess there is also a part of me that doesn't want the marriage to end. As furious as I am with him, I just can't believe that he doesn't still love me. Maybe it could still work.

Pastor: I hear at least two very different sets of feelings and it sounds as if you are caught in a rut, flip-flopping between them. Why don't we look at them one at a time. Let's start where you did, with the feeling of anger. Try to get in touch with those feelings for a few minutes and stay with them. Don't allow yourself to flip back to feelings of wanting to preserve the marriage.

Commentary: This was a good intervention. Whenever a counselor is presented with feelings of ambivalence, the separate feelings should be explored separately and the tendency to flip-flop between them should be resisted.

Karen used this intervention to good profit, first systematically exploring her anger and then her continuing love for her husband.

After further discussion of these matters, the pastor indicated that he believed that she should accept, at least for the moment, her mixed-up feelings and give herself permission to leave them somewhat mixed-up for a while. He then suggested that they return to the question of her intended response to Ken's letter.

Karen: Well, I know I can't keep him in the marriage just because I'm not sure that I want a divorce. He's made up his mind and that really makes the decision for both of us. I guess I need to talk to a lawyer. What do you think?

Pastor: I think that would be a good idea. And at the same time, you might want to discuss with your lawyer Ken's request to come to the house to pick up his remaining personal possessions.

Karen: I'm really uncomfortable with that idea. I don't know if I can trust him. I mean, why should I? Look at how he has deceived me already.

Pastor: I think your caution is well-founded. That is why I suggested discussing this with a lawyer.

Following this interchange, conversation focused on other concerns Karen had about what now seemed to be an inevitable divorce. She was worried that she would not be able to continue to live in their present apartment since her salary would not adequately cover the expense. She also talked about her anxieties about living and being alone. Together they explored her significant relationships and identified several people who seemed to be potentially very good supports for her if she would take the initiative to contact them and let them know what had happened to her. Karen agreed to do this and the pastor told her he would look forward to hearing about these contacts when they next met.

The pastor then returned the discussion to the question of forgiveness.

Pastor: Let's return for a few minutes to the question of forgiveness that we set aside at the beginning of the session. You mentioned that you had begun to develop a list of things for which he needed your forgiveness. Did you bring that with you?

Karen: No, but I can tell you what I put on it. Actually, it was pretty easy. The big thing I have to forgive him for is being a cheat and a liar.

Pastor: That is a big one. But perhaps you can make it more manageable if you focus not on the kind of person he is but on the specific things he has done to hurt you. Forgiveness needs to be for specific offenses, not just for general hurts or for character traits.

Karen: Well, how about that he had an affair and he left me for some other woman? He also lied to me, in fact, he has been living a lie for a long time. And that really hurts. But he began hurting me long before that. He has hurt me so much and so many times that I don't know where to begin. Do I need to tell you every single time he hurt me?

Pastor: No. Even if that were possible, it would take too long and you would be spending too much of your time thinking about your hurt. What I intended for you to do was to write down things as you think of them. In other words, when you feel hurt or anger, turn it into an item on your list, something for which you need to eventually to forgive Ken.

Karen: And then what do I do with the list?

Pastor: The point of the list is to help you prepare to forgive Ken. As you identify things for which you need to forgive him, begin to offer that forgiveness, item by item, as you feel ready. And most important, don't forget to allow God to help you with that process. I would never expect you to be able to forgive Ken by yourself. He doesn't deserve your forgiveness, nor does he seem to be seeking it. To forgive him under those conditions will require God's help.

Karen: That's something I've been thinking about. He doesn't deserve my forgiveness. Shouldn't I wait until he asks for forgiveness, or at least until he shows some signs of feeling sorry for what he has done to me?

Pastor: You could do that, but I'm afraid that if you do you might carry your hurt and anger to your grave. Besides, what if he were to die today? You would be doomed to be a victim of his actions for the rest of your life just because he never came to the point of feeling sorry for what he did. But you do not have to be a victim of these hurts. You do not need to carry their scars with you for the rest of your life. Being free of them does not in any way depend on Ken. It is now something totally between you and God.

Karen: I guess that is good news because I don't really expect he will ever ask my forgiveness. But how is it between me and God? I thought it was between me and Ken.

Pastor: It's primarily between you and God because it isn't dependent on Ken and isn't even something that needs to be communicated to him. It's something that needs to occur in your heart. And for that change of heart, you need God's help. Forgiveness isn't natural for humans. Our natural response is either to retaliate or to save up the right to retaliate and feel sorry for ourselves. Only God can give us an alternative to those two options. Forgiveness is that alternative.

Karen: I know I need God's help. I have been praying that he will help me forgive Ken and I have tried to forgive him for leaving me. But I still feel furious with him. Does that mean that I haven't really forgiven him?

Pastor: Not that you haven't *really* forgiven him but that you haven't yet *totally* forgiven him. Remember that I said that forgiveness is a process. Only God can do it immediately and all at once. The rest of us need to do it a bit at a time and over and over again. Don't be discouraged if you continue to feel hurt and anger or even if you need to forgive him over and over again. Every time you feel a fresh wave of hurt, you will again face the same choice, between harboring the anger and fantasizing revenge or letting go of the anger. Even when you choose to let go of the anger, that is to forgive, you will face the same choice again in the future. Over the coming months, and maybe even years, you will be called upon to let go of that anger many times. This is the process of forgiveness.

The session ended shortly after this. The pastor asked Karen how she had reacted to the book he had given her. She indicated that it had been quite helpful and asked a question which it had raised for her. They discussed this briefly and he suggested that she continue to read the book and note further questions. He also reminded her of her plan to contact several friends and tell them of her circumstances. They together agreed on a time for the next session in four weeks and the pastor suggested to Karen that at this session they would review her progress and consider whether that should be their last formal counseling session or whether one more would be helpful.

Commentary: This session accomplished a good deal. Karen is dealing with her feelings in a responsible way and is making significant progress in her efforts to forgive her husband. The pastor continues to keep the issue of forgiveness in the foreground although quite appropriately, he also continues to discuss feelings and some of the important decisions she is facing. The focus on these decisions and her plans to cope with the changes she was facing brought the sort of concrete behavioral focus to this session which the pastor had intended. Exploration of feelings can be endless unless there is a corresponding focus on behavioral coping. Short-term counseling always requires this behavior focus as a balance to what can otherwise be an endless process of exploring and expressing feelings. The suggestion that they use the next session to review her progress and the related indication that they, at that point, consider whether or not the next session would be the last was the pastor's way of beginning to prepare Karen for the end of their formal work together.

Fourth Session

The pastor began the fourth session by reminding Karen that they had agreed to use this session to review their progress and to further discuss how she was coping. Karen responded by describing her renewed contacts with several friends she hadn't seen for some time. She reported she felt she had pulled back from people in the last six months and now regretted this. Discovering how much these friends really cared for her, she indicated, was beginning to help her feel that there would be life after marriage.

Inquiring about the process of the divorce and further contacts with Ken, the pastor was informed that Karen had contacted an

attorney after their last session and that he was working with Ken's
attorney on the divorce. Karen seemed to feel at peace about this
process, although she was still worried about the financial implications of the dissolution of the marriage. The pastor then asked
Karen how the work of forgiveness was progressing.

Karen: That's really hard. I'm not sure that I've made much progress.
I have tried to forgive him for what he did to me but I'm not
sure I really mean it. Part of me is still really angry at him.

Pastor: I'm not surprised that you are still angry. Remember I told
you that those feelings would probably keep coming up for
some time. Hopefully over time they will be less and less
strong. But you are still pretty close to the hurt so I'm not surprised that the feelings of anger are still strong. The question
is, what do you want to do with those feelings?

Karen: That's easy. I do want to get rid of them. I don't like being
angry. But what Ken did was so unfair. I deserved better than
I got from him.

Pastor: You are absolutely right about that. You did deserve better.
And what he did was cruel and unfair. But that is precisely
why forgiveness is appropriate. If you deserved what you
received, there would be no reason to forgive him.

Karen: But he doesn't deserve forgiveness. He deserves to be hurt
just as he hurt me. He deserves to be punished.

Pastor: Again, I have no argument with that. He does deserve to be
punished, not forgiven. Nobody ever deserves forgiveness.
And that includes me and you.

Karen: (Pause) I think I hear your point. You are saying that I have
received forgiveness and I didn't deserve it either.

Pastor: That's exactly my point. In fact, I believe that is the only reason you could ever be expected to forgive someone else.
Whose forgiveness are you thinking about when you say you
have received forgiveness that you didn't deserve?

Karen: God's. It's pretty clear that I don't deserve his forgiveness and
yet he has given it to me. In fact, he keeps giving it to me even
though I keep sinning. I had never really thought about that
before.

Pastor: One of the reasons for reflecting on God's forgiveness of me when I am trying to forgive someone else is that it reminds me that I am not as different from the person who hurt me as I feel. When I look only at myself and the person who hurt me, I see myself as the victim and them as the villain. I don't feel that we have anything in common. However, when I remember that I, like them, have done things which hurt both God and others, I slowly begin to see myself and the person who hurt me as more alike than I thought. This, I believe, is part of the process of beginning to see the other person through God's eyes, not just through the eyes of my hurt.

Karen: I do want to do that. I have tried to pray for Ken but I haven't felt what you are describing yet.

Pastor: What have you prayed for Ken?

Karen: Well, I've mostly prayed that God would teach him his lesson, that he show him how much he has hurt me.

Pastor: I'm not sure that this is the most important thing you should be praying for. I'd suggest that you begin by praying that God will help you see Ken as he sees him. That is, pray that you would see him with God's love, not your hurt. As God answers this prayer, I think you will begin to see Ken as weak and needy, not simply evil. I think you will begin to catch glimpses of how his own needs, immaturities, and perhaps problems, blinded him to your needs and led him to hurt you. This doesn't excuse what he did. But it might help you understand it.

Karen: I think I see what you are saying. It would really help to see Ken through God's eyes. I can already see how he didn't intend to hurt me. He never really sees beyond himself. That is his problem.

Pastor: And, perhaps, that is something else which you could include in your prayers. But, you should be praying for him, not for him in relationship to yourself. I would suggest that you not pray that he will see how he hurt you (so that you can feel better), but instead that God will help him move beyond his self-preoccupation so that he can be a better person. What you are, in effect, praying as you pray in this manner is that God will bless Ken. That is really the core of the prayer which will change your attitude toward him.

Sensing that Karen might be open to praying such a prayer at that moment, the pastor asked her if she would like to so do. Karen agreed and they prayed asking for God to bless Ken and give her God's love for and perspective on him.

When they finished, Karen stated that she felt much better and indicated that she judged what had just happened to be a turning point for her. Wanting to keep her realistic, the pastor again stated that it was likely that there would be further waves of anger, but that she now had an approach for dealing with these as they would come. He also sensed, however, that she had reached a crucial turning point in her willingness to release this anger and in her ways of relating to God around the hurt.

At the end of this session the pastor asked Karen where she wanted to go from this point. She expressed some of the tentative plans she was developing for her future. The pastor then clarified that what he had intended to ask about was further counseling sessions. She stated that she did not at this point feel that would be necessary but asked if she could call him if she changed her mind. He agreed to this but asked if, in addition, she would call in a month or so, regardless of a mind change, just to let him know how things were going.

Commentary: This seemed to be a natural termination point for the counseling with Karen. She had responded to his somewhat ambiguous inquiry about "where she wanted to go from this point" by talking about her plans for her future. This was a good sign because it indicated that she was moving beyond the point of merely coping with the past to now beginning to deal with her future. Her feelings were much less overwhelming for her and she had made good progress toward forgiving her husband. This work would continue well into the future but this work no longer required continuing counseling sessions.

7

Case Study II

Pastors often think of counseling as an ongoing relationship, failing to realize that it can frequently be conducted within a single session. This is particularly true of Strategic Pastoral Counseling, which, because of its focused nature, is very well suited to the needs of someone who wants a pastoral consultation, not an ongoing counseling relationship. The present case study illustrates the way in which a single-session counseling experience can cover the major tasks of the Strategic Pastoral Counseling model. It is presented to remind pastors of the very significant value of the single-session pastoral consultation.

Bill was a married man in his mid-forties who had been a long-standing member of the church. He and his wife were quite involved in the congregation and their three children had grown up within it. Until recently, he had been an executive with a Christian ministry involved in third world community development and relief work. This position had been terminated at the point of a major reorganization which was necessitated by declining revenues. Bill had received a six-month severance package associated with the termination of his position and during that time he had been able to secure employment with an advertising firm doing work quite similar to that involved in his previous position.

Bill had briefly spoken with the pastor on a couple of occasions about these developments and the present contact began as an after church conversation initiated by the pastor who casually asked him how his job was going. This led to the following:

Bill: The job is going pretty well but I must admit I'm still having a hard time dealing with the way the last one ended.

Pastor: I'm sorry to hear that. In what way are you having a hard time?

Bill: I'm not sure now's the time to get into it. It's a bit hard to explain. Perhaps I should drop by the office some day and talk with you. Do you have any time this week? I don't think it would take long but I would welcome a chance to get some of this off my chest.

Pastor: I have lots of time and would be glad to get together. Why don't you let me give you a call this afternoon and we will set a time to get together early next week.

Commentary: If she were honest, the pastor would have to acknowledge that she had intended the question about work as more of a greeting than a serious inquiry. She was, therefore, somewhat surprised by his response but recovered quickly and asked for more detail. This also didn't produce the intended result as Bill indicated that the time and setting were not right for an answer to her question. This made it clear that he was facing some real struggles and the pastor, still feeling a bit foolish for stumbling unintentionally onto these difficulties, at least felt pleased that she would have an opportunity to deal with them later.

There really is, however, no reason why the pastor should feel badly about this transaction. Bill had not been giving any signals that he was having a problem and small talk, such as she was engaging in, is a necessary part of the social interaction of a church. The only thing which she could have, perhaps, done better in this brief conversation, would have been to replace her question "In what way are you having a hard time?" with a statement such as "I was not aware that this was still a struggle for you." This would have expressed her openness to hear more about the matter without putting him under any demand for specific details.

This is, however, a very small point. The conversation served its purpose in that it sensitized the pastor to Bill's need and allowed them the opportunity to set up a pastoral counseling session.

The session was set for the following Tuesday and in preparation for it the pastor reviewed in her mind what she had heard over the past months about the process of Bill's termination from his former position. Trying to anticipate what might be bothering him, she figured that he might be feeling unfairly treated by his previous employer. Inasmuch as it was a Christian organization, she also wondered if this fact might be the cause of some bitterness or cynicism. She also decided that, in the light of their brief conversation, she would approach the session as if it were to be only a single consultation.

Commentary: This sort of mental rehearsal is quite common, particularly among less experienced pastors. While it is seldom very helpful and usually quite unnecessary (the parishioner will tell you what you need to hear when you get together), in some circumstances it can actually be harmful in that it makes it more difficult to hear what the parishioner says when he or she arrives. Preconceptions can interfere with listening in that it can lead counselors to hear only what they expect to hear. More constructive preparation would be a few moments of prayer for the person, yourself, and your upcoming time together.

The pastor's plan to approach this session as if it were to be only a single consultation was a good one. There was no need to make a firm decision on this now, and in fact, such a firm decision at this point would be inappropriate. However, the immediate indication of the severity of the problem suggested that a single session (or very short-term intervention) might be sufficient. Failure to consider the possibility of a single-session encounter usually leads to the inefficiency of more sessions being employed than would be absolutely necessary. On the other hand, the only potential problem associated with an underestimation of the number of sessions which will be necessary is that the pastor might have to adjust his or her game plan within the first session. Given these possible outcomes, a short-term bias, that is the

tendency to underestimate the total number of necessary sessions,
has fewer potential adverse consequences than a long-term bias.

First Session

Pastor: Good morning Bill. I'm glad to see you.

Bill: Good morning and thanks for taking the time to see me. I'm really glad you asked me about my job. As I said, its going well enough. It's actually pretty similar to what I was doing before. The only difference is that I'm not working for Christians and that's just fine with me. However, the problem isn't my new job. It's my feelings about the old one.

Pastor: Tell me a bit more about that.

Bill: Well, I'm still really upset about how they dumped me. In fact, in some ways I'm more upset now than I was six months ago when it happened. At the time I was told that my termination had nothing to do with me. It was simply a matter of the reorganization, making my whole department redundant. In fact, what they told me was that they would be using external ad agencies to do the work of our department and that this would be more cost-effective for them. They may have done this for a while but what I have since learned is that they recently hired someone to do many of the things I was doing. I don't think this person is at the level I was but it still makes me upset to think that they fired me, telling me it had nothing to do with me, and then turned around and hired someone else to do my job.

Pastor: That really is very upsetting. It must make you feel betrayed. It can't help but look as if they were not being totally straight with you.

Bill: That's it exactly. And they are supposed to be Christians! That's the part that really galls me. That's the last time I will ever work for a Christian organization. I'll take my chances with the wolves any day. Save me from the sheep!

Pastor: It sounds as if a good part of your hurt is your disappointment with how they acted as Christians. You expected more from the ministry because of that fact. You got bit by the sheep and all along you had been led to believe it was the wolves who did the biting.

Commentary: These first few minutes of the session have allowed Bill and the pastor to get well into the tasks of the Encounter stage of Strategic Pastoral Counseling. Because of their prior relationship, joining was immediate. The pastor had done the necessary boundary setting (the specification of the time frame and purpose of the session) during the phone conversation prior to this session. At this point, she had indicated that she had an hour on this morning and that she would look forward to hearing more about his concerns and working with him to try to put them in some sort of a faith perspective. These things being taken care of, this allowed them to move very rapidly into the exploration of the central concern and this was now well under way.

Bill: That's what really hurts. I've worked for a number of Christian organizations and none of them are any better. They all talk a good line but what you see isn't what you get. But this was definitely the worst. If they simply wanted to replace me with someone less expensive, they should have told me that. But where is loyalty? I served them well for four years and did so while taking a big reduction in salary from what I could have been making. That was my commitment to them. Where was their's to me?

Pastor: Good question. But let's bring the focus back to you. Let's go back to why you took the position with the ministry or even, why you did so with previous Christian organizations. I'm interested in hearing about your motivations, expectations, and hopes for working in a Christian organization.

Commentary: This was a very nice intervention. It keeps the focus on Bill, not on his former employer. It also introduces an important historical dimension to his problem and relates appropriately, therefore, to the task of placing the present problems in some sort of historical context. And finally, it introduces a line of discussion which the pastor hopes will help her better understand Bill's spiritual response to his dismissal and the bitterness which he is experiencing.

Bill's response to the pastor's last comment was quite revealing. He indicated that his decision to seek employment in a Christian organization had been motivated by a desire to serve God and make a difference in the world. Prior to the two Christian organizations with which he had served, he had held several jobs in secular advertising firms and had been quite unhappy with his work. These experiences had led him to question the dominant ethics which he saw to be guiding the advertising industry and made him very excited about an opportunity to put his skills to use in a Christian setting.

In response to a question by the pastor about the present state of his motivation to serve God, Bill indicated that he still very much wanted to do this. He also stated that, in contrast to previous secular employment, he felt less value conflict in his present job as he was assigned to only one account, a major hospital, and he had no trouble committing himself to its promotion. However, he also said that he did miss the sense of being directly involved in serving God in his daily work responsibilities. Stating her conviction that service of God was not limited to working in Christian organizations, the pastor encouraged him to discard his distinction between sacred and secular forms of employment and to consider how he could serve God best in and through his present employment.

Bill: I think you are right and I will think some more about that. I really shouldn't feel guilty that I am working where I am. It's a job, and that lets me put bread on the table. And what I am doing is important to the community and, I guess, therefore to God.

Pastor: You are absolutely right about that. But does that make a difference about how you feel regarding your former employer?

Commentary: Quite appropriately the pastor moves the discussion back to the central concern at this point, that is, his continuing upset at the way in which he was treated by the Christian ministry.

Bill: I don't think so. I guess I am still angry at how they treated me.

Pastor: That anger seems pretty reasonable to me. But what do you want to do with it?

Bill: I want to get rid of it. I guess I want to just forget them and not be upset when I think about that whole period of my life.

Pastor: That might well happen with the passing of time but you have another alternative that is more certain in its outcome, but certainly harder. I wonder if you have thought about forgiving the people at the ministry who hurt you.

Bill: I guess that is what I need to do. I have told God that I forgive them but I'm not sure that I meant it. I still feel pretty angry.

Pastor: Who specifically are you angry at? Is it the organization or is it one or more individuals?

Bill: I'm disillusioned with the whole organization, but I guess my anger is really focused on the vice-president to whom I reported. The president wrote me a wonderful letter of reference and really got me my present job. He seemed genuinely sorry to see me leave. I was never sure, however, that this was the case for my boss. You just couldn't tell what he felt. In a lot of ways I never really trusted him.

Pastor: Why was that?

Bill: He just didn't seem trustworthy. He would always say the right things but he was too slippery for me. I had seen how he had treated others in the organization. Nobody really trusted him.

Pastor: Had he ever done anything to you personally that hurt you or made it hard to trust him?

Bill: No, my relationship with him was actually fairly good. Other than quite small things, I never really had any reason to feel angry at him until he told me that along with a number of others, everybody in my advertising department was being let go so the ministry could get out of the red.

Pastor: When you offered him forgiveness earlier, what were you forgiving him for?

Bill: Well, I didn't really think about that. I suppose I was forgiving him for firing me.

Pastor: I think you will find it helpful to be more specific. Let's assume that your dismissal wasn't his idea, that it was part of a plan

Pastor: to cope with the budget deficit developed by the senior managers. If this is a reasonable assumption, we can rule out a simple personal vendetta on his part. Does that seem like a reasonable assumption?

Bill: I have no trouble with that.

Pastor: And yet the way in which he implemented this decision caused you real hurt and anger. So he does bear some responsibility. Some real mistakes were made.

Bill: That's for sure.

Pastor: What were those things that he did or didn't do? If you want to resolve the feelings of hurt and anger you need to forgive him for the specific things he did to hurt you. Let's make a list. What goes on the top of the list?

Bill: Well, that's pretty easy. There is really only one thing on the list. He wasn't totally forthright with me. He owed me a straight explanation. My whole department was closed and two people lost their jobs. He told me that we would be replaced by a contract with an ad agency and that the organization would save $30,000 per year in doing so. This didn't make any sense to me at all and I told him so. And now that they have hired someone else, that just proves my point.

Pastor: Okay. So the most important thing which he did to hurt you was to fire you without having a realistic plan to cope with your dismissal. In fact, it appears that it was so unrealistic that he has now had to turn around and rehire someone else. But earlier you also mentioned the question of loyalty. Is that part of it?

Bill: Well, it wasn't as if I was the only senior person let go. There were a number of others who had worked there much longer than me and one was even a vice-president. But I keep feeling that they owed me something more. Even if they had later called me and told me they had to hire someone for part of the work I had been doing, I would feel like they had treated me more fairly. I think I might have been able to understand that and it would have made me feel like I had been treated with respect.

Pastor: That's an important insight. He hurt you by not treating you with respect, particularly when he subsequently realized that he still needed someone on staff to do at least part of your old job.

Bill: That's it! That's exactly what hurts. And that's precisely why I feel worse about the whole thing than I did a couple of months ago.

Commentary: This part of the session was vitally important if Bill was to be able to let go of his anger and forgive his old boss. To do so, he needed to be clear as to why he was forgiving him. As it now turned out, the real hurt was not so much the initial dismissal as the subsequent hiring of someone to replace him. This fact had been revealed in Bill's second statement at the beginning of the session but the pastor had forgotten it. Bill had probably not forgotten this information but it was only through the process of carefully examining his hurt that he was able to clearly identify the primary and active ingredients in the emotional injury.

Following this, the discussion turned to questions about how to forgive someone who wasn't requesting forgiveness and probably didn't even feel the need for it. Bill also asked whether he needed to talk with his former boss in order to offer this forgiveness. The pastor indicated that forgiveness had to begin as a matter between Bill and God and once he had forgiven the person in his heart, only then would he know whether talking with him would be appropriate. At this point, the pastor asked Bill if he was ready to again offer forgiveness, reminding him that there was a good chance that this might not be the last time he would need to do so. She wondered, however, whether he presently felt prepared to let go of his anger and offer forgiveness.

Bill: I would like to do that. But what am I supposed to do?

Pastor: Well, that is really at the same time the simplest and, yet, the hardest part of the whole process. It's simple because in essence it involves nothing more than giving up your right to remain angry at him. And yet it is also, possibly, the hardest thing a person can be asked to do because everything within us cries out that we have a right to our anger.

Bill: That's for sure. I do feel that somehow it isn't fair that I have
to give up my anger. I know I should but it feels unfair.

Pastor: Nothing in this whole mess has been fair. You were not treated
fairly; there is no question about that. No one has gotten
what they deserve. But your holding onto your anger doesn't
bring about fairness. It doesn't punish your old boss. It only
punishes you. What we learn from God's forgiveness of us
is that forgiveness doesn't have anything to do with fairness.
God's forgiveness of our sins means we don't get what we
deserve. Instead we get what we don't and never could
deserve. Forgiveness cuts through the whole question of just
deserts. And God's forgiveness of us is what makes it possible for us to offer forgiveness to those who hurt us.

Bill: I think I am ready to offer that forgiveness. At least I'd like
to try.

At this point, the pastor suggested that Bill offer this forgiveness
by means of a prayer to God. She also suggested that the thing that
changes a heart of anger to a heart of forgiveness is asking God to
bless the person we are trying to forgive and asking him to help us
see that person as he does, through eyes of love rather than eyes
of hurt. Bill accepted these suggestions and offered a prayer that
reflected them. This was followed by the following interaction.

Bill: That really does begin to change how I view my old boss. Its
hard to pray for a person's blessing and still be angry at him.

Pastor: That's very true and is something you should keep in mind.
You may still have feelings of hurt or anger return, and if you
do, remember how to deal with them. Pray for God's blessing in the life of your old boss and ask God to continue to
heal your hurt.

At this point, the pastor asked Bill if there was anything else he
wished to discuss. Indicating that there was not, they agreed to end
the session. The pastor encouraged him to call her if he wished further help with any of the matters they had discussed. She also gave

him a copy of *Choosing the Gift of Forgiveness*, the book written to accompany this volume but written for counselees.

Commentary: This session illustrates a single-session Strategic Pastoral Counseling intervention around questions of forgiveness. Had things not progressed as well as they did in this session, the pastor would have been quite appropriate in suggesting a subsequent session, perhaps after the passage of several weeks. However, this was not necessary in this situation. Bill has received a good deal of help in less than forty minutes. The help was highly focused, clearly pastoral, explicitly Christian, and carefully attuned to his need.

8

Case Study III

The final case to be presented is that of Jean, an eighteen-year-old member of the congregation who was active in the youth group. Jean was a bright, mature, and highly conscientious girl who was liked by her peers and much respected by the youth pastor. Although she was quiet and somewhat timid in manner, she had been involved with the leadership of the youth group for several years and had been until recently one of its most faithful supporters.

Jean spoke with the youth pastor one night after a Bible study and asked if they could get together to talk sometime. Nancy, her youth pastor, suggested that she pick her up after school the next day and go to a restaurant. Although Nancy had an office at the church, she did the bulk of her counseling in informal settings, finding that this put the kids at ease.

First Session

After picking her up and while driving to a nearby restaurant, the youth pastor initiated a line of casual conversation by asking about school. Jean told her about her involvement in an upcoming school musical and they continued to discuss this and other school activities until they were settled in at the restaurant. At this point the youth pastor asked Jean what it was that she had wanted to discuss.

Jean: Well, its kind of hard to know where to begin. I guess the best place might be the Bible study we had two weeks ago, the one on relationships. You said that night that we can't love another person unless we love ourselves and I guess that's my problem. I don't really even like myself.

Pastor: I'm surprised to hear that, Jean, but I am glad you told me. What is it about yourself that you don't like?

Jean: I just don't like who I am. It's not so much how I look, it more who I am.

Pastor: Help me understand that. What do you mean, it's who you are?

Jean: I don't know if I can. I just don't like myself. I can't really describe it better than that.

Pastor: Let's approach it from a different angle then. Who are you? Suppose you were introducing yourself to someone who didn't know a single thing about you. What would you tell them so that they would know who you were?

Jean: That's really hard. I hate that kind of thing.

Pastor: It is hard, but give it a try. What would you say?

Jean: Well, I guess I'd say that I like people, and I like music and sports. (Pause) I suppose I'd also tell them about my family. But they still wouldn't really know me. No one really does.

Pastor: No one really knows you? A lot of people think they know you and they like the person they think they know. So what is it that they don't know?

Jean: They just don't know me. I'm not the person they see. The person they like is a person I make up. I'm pretty good at playing that role but it isn't me.

Commentary: By this point the pastor was beginning to run out of ideas about how to help Jean express her feelings. And then it struck her that it was feelings she wanted, not formulations about the nature of herself. This led to the following statement.

Pastor: How does it feel to not like yourself so much that you have to play a role so other people will like you?

Jean: Not good. Worse than that. It feels awful. Lately I've been feeling like quitting the youth group. I'm just not the good Christian they all think I am. I'm just not the person I pretend to be.

Commentary: The pursuit of feelings seemed to be no more successful than the pursuit of what it was about herself that she didn't like. The reference to not being a good Christian seemed like a hopeful lead and the pastor now decided to follow this.

Pastor: In what way are you not as good a Christian as you pretend to be?

Jean: I'm just not a very nice person. If you only knew what I sometimes think about my friends. If they only knew . . . I can be the most mean-spirited person around and that's one of the things about myself that I don't like.

Pastor: Your judgement on yourself sounds pretty harsh. But tell me, what is it based on? Who are you thinking about when you describe yourself as mean-spirited?

Jean: You'd use the same words if you knew how I often really feel about my friends. April is a good example. I know I shouldn't be jealous of her but I am. Allan has started going out with her and . . . I guess I have liked him for a long time and he has never even noticed me. It's the same all the time. Everyone likes me as a friend. A friend, yes, but I never have a boyfriend.

Pastor: So you are feeling jealous of April? I can understand that. But you described yourself as mean-spirited.

Jean: I am! Inside I really hate April for being so pretty. I hate her because she has Allan.

Pastor: It sounds as if you are feeling left out. Other girls have boyfriends and all you have are friends who are boys.

Jean: That's true. I do feel left out. And I don't like it.

Commentary: The pastor now feels that she has something concrete to deal with. However, she is unsure if this is the central problem. Jean began by talking about not liking herself and the pastor feels a need to determine how the concern about not hav-

ing a boyfriend relates to these broader feelings of not accepting and liking herself.

Pastor: I understand that you don't have a boyfriend and don't like the feeling of being left out. But you began by talking about not liking yourself. Is this the main thing that you don't like about yourself?

Jean: It's one of them. But I guess what I don't like is that I'm a fake. I know what I am on the inside. Like I said, I'm awful and mean. And not just around April. I think awful things about lots of my friends. And sometimes I don't just think them. (Long pause)

Pastor: What do you mean you "don't just think them"?

Jean: I don't think I'm ready to talk about that. I wish I hadn't said that.

Pastor: You don't have to say anything more than you want. But you are talking about not being real, of playing some kind of a role. I'd like to invite you, when you feel ready, to be perfectly honest with at least one person—me. I accept that you think and do things that are far from Christian and I don't like you any less now that I know that about you. In fact, I really respect you for your honesty in telling me.

Jean: (Beginning to cry) I want to tell you, but I'm just so ashamed of myself. (Long pause) I started a rumor at school about April and I feel so sorry now. I did it just to hurt her and I know it did. But I don't know what to do about it. I told some of her friends that April had an abortion. I told them that I heard it from my parents who are good friends of her parents. Her friends believed me. I know that, because they told others. I heard the rumor from two different people so I know it got around. And I know April heard it too. She doesn't know who started it but I know she was really hurt. And it wasn't true. I made it up just to hurt her because I was jealous of her.

Pastor: What you did was wrong. You know that. But when you tell me what you did, it helps me understand just how jealous you are of April. It also helps me understand just how badly you must be feeling about yourself.

Jean: (Crying) You don't have any idea how badly I feel. What I did was unforgivable. How can I call myself a Christian? How can I pretend I am her friend? Now you see why I want to drop out of the group. (Sobbing)

By this point Jean's crying had become rather noticeable and the pastor was wishing she had chosen a less public place to meet. She asked Jean if she would like to continue talking in the restaurant or if she wanted to go back to the church to her office. Jean said that she didn't want to talk about it anymore and wanted to go home. The pastor stated that she hated to leave Jean at this point and asked if she wouldn't reconsider coming back to the church. Jean reaffirmed that she wished to go home. The pastor said she would call her later that night and that she wanted to get together again soon.

Commentary: This was the first time the youth pastor had encountered a problem in choosing to meet adolescents in restaurants or other public settings. However, while she wished she had seen Jean at the church or somewhere more private, she did not feel that her basic plan of generally meeting kids somewhere other than the church was incorrect.

She was, however, very troubled about Jean. She felt her pain and felt that she had been unable to do anything to help her. In reality, however, she had. She had allowed Jean the opportunity to express her pain and pain expressed to another person is pain shared. This was a start for Jean for now she had at least shared her feelings with someone. The pastor's hope was that they could continue the discussion soon and that she would be able to help Jean experience the forgiveness and love of God.

The pastor called Jean later that evening and asked how she was feeling. Jean apologized for becoming so upset and said that was feeling better. The pastor suggested that they get together the next day and talk further and Jean agreed, indicating that perhaps they should meet at her office at the church. Jean also told the pastor that there was something else she wanted to tell her but had been afraid. She said she would try and tell her when they met the next day.

Second Session

Jean arrived at the church the following day after school looking quite upset. She began the session by repeating that she had a secret but that she didn't feel ready to share it. The pastor told her that she respected her sense of timing but hoped Jean could feel safe enough to share this secret with her.

Commentary: Secrets of this sort are not at all uncommon with adolescents. They represent a real trap if the counselor becomes focused on them, trying to get the adolescent to tell their secret. The pastor, noting that Jean began the session by referring to this secret, is aware that it is a preoccupying concern for her. However, she wisely decides to avoid trying to pry it out of her and decides to return to the discussion of the previous day.

Pastor: If you are willing I'd like to suggest that we return to your judgment that starting the rumor about April places you beyond God's forgiveness. Tell me a bit more about that.

Jean: It was an awful thing to do. I set out to hurt her and that's exactly what I did. She had a clean reputation and I ruined it for her. She would never get pregnant and if she did, she would never have an abortion. (Beginning to cry) She just isn't like that. (Pause)

Pastor: You could have hurt her reputation in a lot of different ways. Why did you make up a story about an abortion?

Jean: (Beginning to sob uncontrollably) That's my secret. That's what threatened to ruin my reputation. (Long pause) Please don't ever tell anyone what I am going to tell you. Last summer I got pregnant and I had an abortion. Now you know why I hate myself. I could never forgive myself for what I did. It's awful! I'm awful!

Commentary: This sudden disclosure of the secret which Jean had been protesting she wasn't ready to share caught the pastor totally off guard. However, immediately, the pieces of the puzzle fell into place. Why Jean hated herself, why she had started the rumor about her friend, why she felt so phony as a Christian,

*why she was thinking about dropping out of the youth group—
all these matters seemed clearly linked to her pregnancy and the
subsequent abortion. The pastor also realized that she had been
quite worried about Jean the previous summer, as she had seemed
depressed and withdrawn. This had seemed to pass after a few
months and she now regretted that she had not taken more initiative in seeking her out during this period.*

The pastor's response to this disclosure was to get out of her
chair and go and hug Jean, assuring her of her love for her and her
sorrow about the tremendous burden she now knew Jean had car-
ried alone for so long. Jean continued to sob deeply and neither
spoke for several moments. As her crying began to subside somewhat, the pastor returned to her chair.

Pastor: Jean, now I think I am beginning to understand why you hate
yourself so much. The incident with April is just a small tip of
the iceberg. You must feel overwhelmed with guilt.

Jean: I do. I just feel so ashamed of myself. It just seems like a bad
dream. I can't believe it really happened. I can't believe I had
sex, I can't believe I got pregnant, and I can't believe what I
did . . . I mean the abortion.

Pastor: Why don't you walk me through that sequence in a little more
detail? I know it might be difficult but I think it is important
that you talk the whole thing through.

Jean proceeded to describe the events of the past six months.
They began with a single sexual experience, her first and last, which
occurred after a party where she had gotten drunk. Jean was not
accustomed to either attending such parties or drinking. However,
this event was part of her high school graduation and she found herself caught up in things she had always rejected for herself. Although
her memory of the evening was unclear, she recalled deciding to
throw caution and principles to the wind and have a good time. She
also recalled her date pressing her for sex in his car after the party
and recalled giving in to this and passing out soon thereafter.

The next day she felt overwhelmed with guilt and worry. She felt
deeply ashamed of what she had done and worried about her rep-

utation and about becoming pregnant. Her school friends teased her about getting drunk, but no one seemed aware of anything else having occurred between her and her date. Given that her friends were all dispersing after the summer, she hoped that maybe she could keep the events of that night secret. She tried to seek God's forgiveness and forget about the whole matter. However, this all fell apart when she discovered she was pregnant.

At this point, her resolve to cover up the whole matter was almost automatic. She gave no serious consideration to telling either her parents, her date (who she hadn't even seen since that night), or even her closest friend and made her decision to proceed with an abortion after only a very short period of agony. However, her agony wasn't resolved with this action; the guilt and self-loathing were just about to begin. As Jean began to describe the depth of these feelings, she stated that she could never forgive herself for what she had done and that she also could never again ask for or accept God's forgiveness. This led to the following interaction:

Pastor: Jean, I have no doubt about how badly you feel because of what you have done. But I don't agree that this places you outside God's forgiveness or his love for you.

Jean: Haven't you been listening to me? I threw away everything I stood for, including my commitment to follow Jesus. And then I killed the life that was within me. If God can overlook that, I don't think he is the kind of God I can respect.

Pastor: But God doesn't overlook what you have done. He agrees with you when you affirm that it was wrong. What you did was sinful and sin deserves punishment. But Christ has taken the punishment for your sin. That is why God can offer you his forgiveness. He isn't overlooking what you have done. He's telling you that those sins, along with all the others you have ever or will ever commit, are the reason Jesus died.

Jean: I guess I know that but I can't accept it. Since then, I don't want God's love or his forgiveness. I feel I don't deserve it.

Pastor: Again, you are absolutely right about that. You don't deserve his love or his forgiveness. But whether you accept it or not, it is there for you. He does love you and he hurts with you as you have been crushed with these feelings for the past six months. I really believe that. If I feel your pain to some extent and if I hurt along with you, this is just a small fraction of how closely Jesus identifies with you in your hurt. He doesn't stand over you shaking his finger and hoping you feel terrible. He stands beside you, crying with you and hoping you will receive his love and forgiveness.

Jean: (Crying) I guess I do really want that but I don't think I can forgive myself.

Pastor: Perhaps that's the real problem. You are so angry at yourself for what you did that you can't stand the thought of being forgiven.

Jean: I am angry. I'm disgusted. I can hardly look at myself in the mirror. That's why I keep thinking that the whole thing was a bad dream. Everything I thought I knew about myself now seems like a lie. I don't know who I really am. The person I thought I was certainly wouldn't have done the things I did.

Pastor: But that's where you are wrong. All of us are capable of inconceivable sin and wickedness. That's why I don't feel disgusted by what you have told me. I know that I, too, could do the same or worse. God knows the sinfulness of human nature. It hurts him when we sin but I'm convinced it doesn't shock him. It seems that God is more realistic about your sinfulness than you are.

The session ended shortly after this. The youth pastor closed the session by praying for Jean, asking that God would assure her of his love and help her receive his forgiveness and her own. She then gave her the companion volume on forgiveness and asked her to begin reading it to see if it would provide any help with her struggles around self-forgiveness. The pastor also suggested that Jean reflect on what made her so special that of all the people who had lived and sinned, her sins alone were so bad that they could not be covered by the death of Christ. She agreed to reflect on this and to meet again in two weeks.

Commentary: This was obviously a very important session and the pastor felt good that finally they had gotten to the core of

Jean's problems. In this session, the pastor demonstrated a high degree of skill in empathizing in a nonjudgmental way with Jean. Jean knew what she had done was wrong and needed no further reminders of this. But experiencing her pastor's love rather than judgment would help her receive the same from God. And if she was to forgive herself, it would be absolutely essential that she first accept God's forgiveness of her.

Third Session

The youth pastor saw Jean twice, very briefly, between the second and third sessions and, although they did not talk about any of the matters they had discussed privately, Jean did say that things had been going better. When she arrived for the third session, also held at the church, she started with the same assertion.

Jean: A lot has happened since we last talked and I have really been looking forward to seeing you again. The book you gave me was really helpful. I read it all in a couple of days and have been going back through it and rereading parts of it. But the most helpful thing was your comment just as I was leaving. You told me to reflect on what made me so special that God couldn't forgive me. At first I felt angry that you said that. It felt like you didn't really accept how bad what I did was. I didn't want you to tell me that what I had done was okay and I know you didn't. But at the time, it sounded like this. However, the more I thought about what you said, the more I realized that I was setting myself in some special class of the world's absolute worst sinners. And while I feel like that, I know that isn't true.

Pastor: I'm really glad you have begun to come to that realization. What you did was bad. But that's just precisely the reason Jesus had to die.

Jean: I think I am beginning to see that. I always thought of myself as basically okay. Not that I didn't sin, but nothing really big. This past summer sure blew that illusion away! I'm really rotten. And I guess that admitting that changes how I have to look at myself a lot.

Pastor: What do you mean by that?

Jean: Well I used to feel pretty proud of myself. Not that I liked everything about myself, but I guess I sort of felt morally superior to most of my friends. I would secretly feel smug when they did things I disapproved of, even though I never let them know how I felt.

Pastor: Maybe you also felt some jealousy of them.

Jean: Maybe you are right. I never thought about it that way but nothing would surprise me now. (Pause) In fact, I think you might be right. I suppose I did feel jealous about the fun they seemed to have. But that makes me really mad because lots of people have sex and never get pregnant. That really doesn't seem fair. I mean, I only did it once and look what happened to me.

Commentary: At this point, the pastor faces an important decision, whether or not to respond to Jean's question about the fairness of her pregnancy. She wisely decides to ignore this question, not because it is not important but because it does not seem to be a central issue. If anger at God turns out to be more prominent than now appears to be the case, she may have to return to this issue later. However, at present the pastor determines that she wants to hear more about Jean's awareness of her jealousy of her non-Christian friends.

The reason the jealousy seems important is that the pastor hopes that it will prove helpful in assisting Jean in taking responsibility for her behavior. The pastor's goal is to help her see that it wasn't simply a matter of "something having come over her" on the fateful night of the party. Rather, Jean made a series of choices which had their roots in the way she was feeling and behaving prior to this night. While the pastor's central goal is to help Jean forgive herself for what she had done, it is also her goal to help Jean learn from what had happened. Simply saying, "I'll never get myself into that sort of a situation," is not satisfactory. Rather, the pastor hopes Jean will be able to learn why she got herself into the situation, and by coming to know herself better, avoid future experiences of fooling herself and getting into trouble.

Pastor: Let's go back to the question of your feeling jealous of your friends. The reason I think this is important is that feelings, such as this, can be very strong, and, particularly if you are unable to acknowledge them, such feelings can influence your behavior in ways that go beyond your awareness. I guess what I'm saying is that I think those feelings of jealousy were an important part of why you got into trouble that night. Do you agree?

Jean: Do you mean that because I was secretly jealous of the fun my non-Christian friends seemed to be having, I did what I did?

Pastor: Something like that.

Jean: Well, maybe I did but what difference does it make?

Pastor: I think it makes a big difference. Did you get attacked by some kind of a demon of drunkenness and sex or did you choose to do what you did? I guess I'm asking that to help you learn from what happened. What do you think?

Jean: I think I see where you are going with that and I guess I'd have to say that I chose to do what I did. Not that I thought it through very carefully, but if I am honest, I'd have to say that I decided to get drunk and be wild that night. I just wanted to let it all go and give it a try. Everyone else seemed to do it all the time. I wanted to get a part of the action. I was tired of standing on the sidelines.

Pastor: That's a very honest self-assessment. I really respect you for being able to be so honest. I think that is the beginning of really dealing with what has happened.

Jean: Well, I have to be honest. I'm tired of trying to fool myself and others. That's what I meant when I said I was tired of pretending to be a Christian.

Pastor: It is time for you to become more honest. But that doesn't mean you have to stop being a Christian. A better choice, in my judgment, is to choose to try to be a more honest Christian, that is, honest first and foremost with God, then with yourself, and then with others. But the place where you learn this honesty is with God. Being honest with him is the start to being honest everywhere else.

Jean: I do want to do that. You are right. I haven't been very honest with God or myself. I've tried to look like I thought I was supposed to look. I remember hearing somebody talk about how to be successful you have to "fake it until you make it." I understood that very clearly. That's how I have always approached the Christian life. It never struck me that there was any alternative to that. But I am beginning to feel that if there isn't an alternative, I'm not sure I want to be a Christian.

Pastor: I'm really glad to hear that you are ready to give up that sort of phony Christianity. There is an alternative. You don't have to "fake it until you make it." And I am very excited to see you open to learning what that alternative is.

Commentary: This was a very good series of interventions on the part of the pastor who here shows herself to be quite a skilled counselor. She is capable of being highly directive and quite confrontive, the latter seen particularly in the way in which she introduces the question of Jean's lack of honesty. She is also courageous when she affirms the health of Jean's desire to give up the "fake it until you make it" approach to the Christian life which she has lived to the present. Some Christian counselors get nervous at this point, becoming afraid of the risks of a person giving up, not just the unhealthy aspects of faith, but faith entirely. While this is always a danger, the costs of settling for a pathological form of faith, such as Jean had been describing, are extremely high. The pastor correctly noted that Jean wasn't fed up with Christianity, just with her dishonest ways of being a Christian.

This line of discussion continued for another ten minutes. Judging that Jean clearly understood at least the broad outlines of living more honestly before her God, the pastor sought to return the focus to the question of forgiveness.

Pastor: Learning to be honest with God and with yourself about what you are feeling won't happen overnight. But don't let yourself settle for anything less than this. Anything less isn't Christianity. But another vital part of the Christian life is receiving

forgiveness for our sins and I want to check back to that matter and hear where you feel you now stand in terms of receiving forgiveness for what you did.

Jean: Well, I have asked God to forgive me and I guess he has, but I'm not doing so well forgiving myself.

Pastor: Let's start with what you have been able to receive forgive-ness for. What does that include?

Jean: For deciding to give the wild life a try. I think he has forgiven me for that.

Pastor: Anything else?

Jean: I guess that includes getting drunk and maybe even having sex. But what I can't accept is the abortion. That's the part I feel the worst about. That's the part I can't forgive and can't ask God to forgive.

Pastor: As I asked before, what makes that such an awful sin that the death of Jesus can't cover it?

Jean: That's not the point. I think God could forgive me for that. I can't forgive myself. I can't ask him for forgiveness. All my life I've stood against abortion. I just don't believe in it. But look what I did. I am such a hypocrite. That's what I can't stand.

Pastor: Once again, you are absolutely right in being disgusted with hypocrisy. Jesus felt the same when he was on earth. But that isn't the point. The point is not whether you are a hypocrite but what you are going to do about it. Remember when I said that nothing that you could do would surprise God? He isn't surprised by hypocrisy or any other sin. He simply asks us to come to him for forgiveness when we commit sins and ask for his help to resist such sins in the future. He doesn't expect us to be sinless. If we were, Jesus wouldn't have had to die.

Jean: But I just can't forgive myself.

Pastor: Can't or won't?

Jean: Maybe it's won't.

Pastor: Why won't you allow yourself to experience forgiveness for what you did?

Jean: I guess I feel a need to be punished.

Pastor: I think that's it exactly. You want to pay for your sins. You resist the idea of letting Jesus pay. You think you'd feel better if you pay at least something. Maybe, you think that feeling miserable for a little longer will partially atone for what you did.

Jean: When you put it that way it sounds pretty ridiculous but that is pretty close to how it feels. I just feel like I need to pay something for what I did.

Pastor: The point is, the penalty for what you did is much higher than you realize. The penalty for sin of any sort isn't feeling badly for a period of time. It isn't even doing good deeds or doing without some desired things for the rest of your life. The penalty for sin is death. That's the penalty for any sin, even a single one.

Jean: Well there have certainly been times when I felt prepared to pay that penalty. I don't now but after it first happened, I really thought about killing myself. I'd have been happy to pay that penalty.

Pastor: But the point is that your efforts to atone for your sins are useless. That's why you need to throw yourself on God's mercy and accept his forgiveness.

Jean: Well, I'm a lot closer to that point than I was the last time I saw you. It's just hard. It's hard to stop punishing myself for what I did.

Pastor: I know that it is.

The session ended shortly after this, the pastor again encouraging Jean to continue to read the book on forgiveness and suggesting several passages of Scripture to study. The pastor also suggested that she would like Jean to reflect on what she needed to do to resolve the situation with her friend, April, the girl about whom she had started the unfounded rumor. Jean agreed to think about this before the next session which was set for four weeks hence. The pastor suggested that they approach this next session as if it would be the last, although she also indicated that if they determined that another one was needed after this, that would also be fine.

Commentary: This was a very profitable session. Jean is making real progress in her movement toward receiving forgiveness for the things she did and has also taken some marked steps toward learning from the whole experience. Her faith seems stronger and her relationship with God healthier.

The decision to return to the question of her relationship with April was a good one. Dealing with the past starts between the individual and God but often involves other parties. In Jean's case, the pastor felt strongly that she needed to seek April's forgiveness if she was to really take a significant step toward not only resolving the past but toward a future based on more honesty and integrity.

Fourth Session

Jean began the fourth session by stating that she had thought a lot about what they discussed the last time and that it all really made sense. She also said that after much soul-searching, she had decided to talk to April and had done so the previous week. Although she had approached this with great fear, April had seemed to understand and offered Jean her forgiveness. Jean hadn't told her about her own abortion, but had told her about her long-standing jealousy. The encounter seemed to be very healing for Jean. Where it left April was unknown and the youth pastor, knowing her through the youth group, hoped that April would initiate conversation with her about it at some point.

Jean then indicated that dealing with the abortion was much harder. The pastor asked what she meant by this.

Jean: I just mean that I feel awful about what I did. I keep thinking about it. I keep thinking about the little baby I killed. I wonder what he or she would look like and how I would feel as a mother. I just feel really sad about what I did.

Pastor: It sounds to me as if what you are feeling about the abortion has changed a bit from when we last talked. Then it seemed to me you were primarily angry at yourself for what you had done. You felt a need to be punished for what you did, a need to atone for your sins. Now it sounds more like sadness.

Jean: I guess I'm just really confused. I feel all of that. Although lately, I'm mostly sad.

Pastor: Tell me more about that.

Jean: I just feel sad. And I'm full of regret. At the time I thought the absolute worst thing in the world had happened to me when I got pregnant. Now I sometimes wish I had kept the baby. I think I might have liked it. I know it would have changed my life, but I could have handled that and maybe I'd have liked it. Maybe it's what I should have done.

Pastor: It's hard to know and probably not all that helpful after the fact to try and second-guess the matter. But it sounds to me as if what you are experiencing is grief. Up until recently you never allowed yourself to experience anything but anger at yourself. But you lost something, probably a number of things. In more ways than one, you lost some parts of yourself. And it appears to me that you are now beginning to grieve over those losses.

Jean: It's funny you should use that word. That's just what I came to call it this last week. It feels like I have lost something. And I'm just really sad.

Pastor: Let's talk about what you have lost. How would you describe the things you have lost through this experience?

Jean: Well, first of all I have lost my childhood. And my innocence. In one night, I lost my virginity and within a month or so, I lost anything that was left of innocence when I had the abortion. It all happened so fast. I wish I could go back to last spring and relive the last eight months. I'd do everything so different.

Pastor: I'm sure you would, but let's stick with this question of what else you have lost.

Jean: (Pause) I guess I also lost my reputation. Not that everybody knows what I did, but a lot of people know that I got bombed out of my mind that night and Rick, my date, knows that I had sex with him. I'm so glad I've never seen him since then. I don't think I could face him. He left for a summer job out of state the next week and in September he went to a college on the East Coast. If I'm lucky, I'll never see him again.

Pastor: What do you mean that you lost your reputation?

Jean: I had a good reputation and now I don't. People know that I'm not the goody-goody I pretended to be.

Pastor: But that's true. You aren't what you pretended to be.

Jean: But I did things a Christian shouldn't do. I hurt God's reputation, not just mine.

Pastor: That's a different matter and a very good point. That is something to feel sorry about.

Jean: I do, and I have asked God to forgive me for that. But I still feel sorry for how I behaved.

Pastor: What else have you lost?

Jean: A baby. That's what doesn't make any sense but like I said, I really feel sad about the little life I took. (Beginning to cry) Sometimes I dream about babies. I never used to do that, but I find myself thinking about them too. And if I'm out somewhere and I see a woman with a baby, I just feel really sad. And it makes me think about the baby I was carrying and I feel even worse.

Commentary: This discussion made clear to the pastor that Jean was experiencing a grief reaction to the various losses associated with the events of the past months. She also felt that she was not going to be able to help her resolve these feelings in the present session. Correctly, she concluded that work on these issues would require a number of sessions and that such work was different enough from what had been their focus to this point (centering on forgiveness and learning from the experience) that it constituted a new counseling contract. She decided, therefore, to suggest that Jean see another counselor who could work with her around these issues. This would then allow her to bring some closure to the work they had done together on forgiveness and not allow this focus to be diluted by moving to something quite different even if related.

The pastor suggested the idea of a referral to Jean who was, surprisingly, open to it. She told Jean that dealing with grief was an area of special interest of a friend of hers who worked in a nearby Christian counseling clinic and that she would be glad to make the referral and help her get started. Jean agreed, asking, however, if that meant that she wouldn't see the pastor any longer.

Pastor: Not at all! In fact, I would really hope that we could get together every now and then so you could fill me in on how things are going. But it seems to me we are winding down the regular counseling sessions. That stage of our work together seems to me to be coming to a close. But I do hope we can still keep in close touch. Does that seem okay to you?

Jean: That seems fine. I would like to get together and talk. After all, nobody else knows as much about me as you do.

Pastor: Well, let's count on that. But before we finish I would like to review where we have come from and see if there are any other loose ends that we need to take care of. Perhaps, to do that I could ask you to reflect back on the weeks since we first met and tell me what you have learned. What's better, what's the same, and if anything is worse, you'd better tell me about that as well! (laughing)

This led to a review of their work together. Jean stated that she had come to accept and feel God's forgiveness and most of the time she was also prepared to forgive herself for what she did. She then talked at length about how she was learning to be more honest in her relationships. She was finding this hard but, for the most part, more satisfying than her old patterns. She stated that her prayers were much more honest and real; God, in turn, also seemed more real.

In response to the pastor's question about whether she liked herself any better now (this having been the presenting problem), Jean stated that she wasn't sure that she did but she liked the direction things were going. She then returned to a discussion of her sadness.

At this point the pastor felt there was no advantage to using the small amount of time remaining to further explore these feelings and, consequently, resolved to end the session by trying to give Jean some hope for her continuing work around these matters. She asked if they could pray together and they did so. They then hugged and agreed to get together at the restaurant were they first met sometime soon after her first session with the new counselor. Jean was to take responsibility to set this time up once the first appointment at the clinic was established, and left quite happy with these arrangements.

Commentary: Some readers will feel the pastor should not have referred Jean but rather continued with her for the additional work that was necessary. Let's review the reasons why this pastor did as she did. First, she was aware of someone else who could provide this counseling at least as well as she and probably better. Second, this then allowed her to return to her more ongoing role of youth pastor for Jean. While working together in an intensive counseling mode, it is difficult to fulfill other regular pastoral responsibilities to the person. Nancy (the youth pastor) had often felt somewhat awkward when encountering Jean at the church. Should they make any reference to their private work together or pretend it wasn't occurring? This is always the dilemma and as such, counseling represents a potential complication to other pastoral ways of relating to a parishioner.

In other circumstances, it might be appropriate for the pastor to shift the focus and begin to deal with the problems of grief. However, if this is done, it is best to finish the present course of counseling, take a break, and start over with a new focus and a new time limit.

Pastoral counselors must continuously guard against short-term counseling relationships drifting into ongoing, long-term ones. If counseling is going well, few counselees ever object to such a drift. The effort to minimize such drift must, therefore, remain with the counselor. The time pressures and variety of role demands of pastors make such vigilance crucial. The present case illustrates how it can be done.

Notes

Chapter 1: The Importance of Forgiveness

1. Dan D. Allender, *The Wounded Heart* (NavPress, Colorado Springs: 1990), p. 61.

2. E. M. Pattison, "On the Failure to Forgive or be Forgiven," *American Journal of Psychotherapy*, 31(1):106–115.

3. Richard E. Ecker, "Whatever happened to grace?" *Perspectives*, March 1992, Vol. 7, Number 3, p. 14.

4. Dennis and Matthew Linn, *Healing Life's Hurts: Healing Memories Through the Five Stages of Forgiveness* (New York: Paulist, 1979), p. 151.

5. R. Lofton Hudson, *"Grace Is Not a Blue-Eyed Blond"* (Waco, Texas: Word, 1972), p. 72 (quoted in: *Forgiveness*, Dan Hamilton [Downers Grove: InterVarsity Press, 1980], p. 6).

6. Whereas Genesis 50:26 reminds us of Genesis 3:19, the first judgment on sin, Genesis 50:15–21 reminds us of 3:15, the first promise of salvation.

7. Lyman T. Lundeen, "Forgiveness and Human Relationships," in *Counseling and the Human Predicament*, ed. by Leroy Aden and David G. Benner (Grand Rapids: Baker Book House, 1989), p. 188.

8. Lundeen, p. 180.

9. Lundeen, pp. 184, 196.

10. Lundeen, pp. 191–92.

11. Gregg Lewis. "Broken, But Forgiven," *Marriage Partnership Magazine*, Spring 1988, p. 93.

Chapter 2: The Possibility of Forgiveness

1. Jay Kesler, *Being Holy, Being Human* (Waco: Christianity Today, Inc. and Word, Inc., 1988), p. 49.

2. G. C. Berkhouwer, *Sin* (Grand Rapids: Wm. B. Eerdmans Publishing Co., 1971), p. 387.

3. Berkhouwer, p. 392.

4. Lous Berkhof, *Summary of Christian Doctrine* (Grand Rapids: Wm. B. Eerdmans Publishing Company, 1938).

5. Walter Wangerin Jr., *As For Me and My House* (Nashville: Thomas Nelson Publishers, 1990), pp. 90–91.

6. Wangerin, pp. 90–91.

7. David G. Benner, *Healing Emotional Wounds* (Grand Rapids: Baker Book House, 1990), p. 102.

8. Roger Lundin, "The Ultimately Liveral Condition," *First Things*, April 1995, p. 25.

9. M. Scott Peck, *The People of the Lie*, quoted in *From Fear to Freedom*, Rose Marie Miller (Wheaton: Harold Shaw Publishers, 1994), p. 85.

10. David G. Benner, *Healing Emotional Wounds* (Grand Rapids: Baker Book House, 1990), pp. 91–92.

Chapter 3: The Necessity of Forgiveness

1. Editorial, *The New Yorker Magazine*, January 29, 1990, p. 25.
2. Ibid.
3. Dennis Guernsey, *Sometimes It's Hard to Love God* (Downers Grove: InterVarsity Press, 1989), pp. 142–43.
4. William G. Justice, Jr., *Guilt and Forgiveness* (Grand Rapids: Baker Book House, 1980), p. 91.
5. See pages 44–49 of David G. Benner's *Healing Emotional Wounds* (Baker Book House, 1990) for further discussion of these masks of anger.
6. Allender, *Wounded Heart*.
7. Lewis B. Smedes, *Forgive and Forget* (San Francisco: Harper and Row, 1984), p. 29.
8. Lyman T. Lundeen, *Counseling and the Human Predicament*, ed. Leroy Aden and David G. Benner (Grand Rapids: Baker Book House, 1989), p. 181.
9. Smedes, pp. 106–107, 113.
10. S. Bruce Narramore, "Guilt: Where Theology and Psychology Meet," in *Wholeness and Holiness*, ed. H. Newton Malony (Grand Rapids: Baker Book House, 1983), p. 234.
11. David G. Benner, *Strategies of Pastoral Counseling* (Grand Rapids: Baker Book House, 1992), p. 21.

Chapter 4: The Difficulty of Forgiveness

1. Smedes, pp. 141–42.
2. Lundeen, pp. 178–80.
3. Richard P. Lord, "Do I Have to Forgive?", *The Christian Century*, Ocotober 9, 1991, pp. 902–903.
4. Leon Morris, *The Atonement* (Downers Grove: InterVarsity Press, 1983), pp. 199–200.
5. For more on this and other sources of resistance to forgiveness, see chapter 5 of David G. Benner, *Healing Emotional Wounds*, pp. 113–17.
6. Lundeen, pp. 190–91.
7. Wangerin, p. 81.
8. Rinda G. Rogers, "Forgiveness and the Healing of the Family," in *Counseling and the Human Predicament*, ed. Leroy Aden and David G. Benner (Grand Rapids: Baker Book House, 1989), pp. 198–200.
9. Dan Hamilton, *Forgiveness* (Downers Grove: InterVarsity Press, 1980), pp. 22–23.
10. Wangerin, p. 100.
11. J. I. Packer, *Rediscovering Holiness* (Ann Arbor: Servant Publications, 1992), p. 93.

Chapter 5: The Role of Forgiveness in Pastoral Care

1. For a more complete discussion of the dynmaics of emotional wounds and the therapeutic process involved in their healing, see *Healing Emotional Wounds* by David G. Benner (Baker Book House, 1990).
2. For further discussion of shame and guilt and a Strategic Pastoral Counseling response to these problems see Daniel Green and Mel Lawrenz, *Encountering Shame and Guilt* (Grand Rapids: Baker, 1994).
3. Philip Yancey, *Disappointment with God* (Grand Rapids: Zondervan, 1988).